TO BE
AWAY

E UROP

A

Unity (

As Europe moves towards economic and political unification, many wonder why legal unification makes so little headway. In this concise but wide-ranging book, R. C. Van Caenegem considers the historical reasons behind this legal diversity. He stresses the importance of the adoption on the Continent – but not in England – of the classical law of the Romans, and shows how the rise of the nation states led to a multitude of national codes of law. The impact of politics on legal development is another key factor, and as a graphic example Van Caenegem provides a detailed account of how the German past was extolled in Nazi Germany.

The book concludes with a consideration of the ongoing debate on the desirability – indeed, on the possibility – of European legal unification and of a federal constitution for a united Europe. —

R. C. VAN CAENEGEM is Professor Emeritus in the Faculty of Law and the Faculty of Letters, University of Ghent. His many publications include *The birth of the English common law* (1973; second edition 1988), *Judges, legislators and professors* (1987), *An historical introduction to private law* (English language edition 1992) and *An historical introduction to Western constitutional law* (1995).

EUROPEAN LAW IN THE PAST AND THE FUTURE

Unity and Diversity over Two Millennia

PROFESSOR R. C. VAN CAENEGEM

University of Ghent

CAMBRIDGE
UNIVERSITY PRESS

PUBLISHED BY THE PRESS SYNDICATE OF THE UNIVERSITY OF CAMBRIDGE
The Pitt Building, Trumpington Street, Cambridge, United Kingdom

CAMBRIDGE UNIVERSITY PRESS
The Edinburgh Building, Cambridge CB2 2RU, UK
40 West 20th Street, New York, NY 10011-4211, USA
477 Williamstown Road, Port Melbourne, VIC 3207, Australia
Ruiz de Alarcón 13, 28014 Madrid, Spain
Dock House, The Waterfront, Cape Town 8001, South Africa

http://www.cambridge.org

© R. C. Van Caenegem 2002

First published 2002

Printed in the United Kingdom at the University Press, Cambridge

Typeface Baskerville Monotype 11/12.5 pt.   *System* LaTeX 2$_\varepsilon$ [TB]

A catalogue record for this book is available from the British Library

ISBN 0 521 80938 X hardback
ISBN 0 521 00648 1 paperback

Contents

Preface

In recent years I have had the privilege of teaching a course
on European legal history in the Magister Iuris Communis Programme in the University of Maastricht. The classes were small
and consisted of students who had already obtained degrees in
Law at home. They came from various countries and continents,
from Sweden to Brazil and from Ireland to Iran, and were a re-
ceptive audience, whom it was a pleasure to teach. Nor did they
only listen, but they also asked interesting questions and engaged
in lively debates.

The present book is the outcome of those Maastricht lectures
and owes much to the suggestions and questions which were
put to me by the students and also to the discussions I had
with my colleagues in the Maastricht Law Faculty, who took a
particular interest in the European legal past and the possibility
of a common European law of the future. One of these colleagues
I would like especially to name here is Professor Nicholas Roos,
who took the initiative of entering European legal history in
the Magister Iuris Communis Programme and of inviting me to
lecture on it. To all of them I express my warmest thanks.

The present book does not attempt to give a general survey,
but merely presents a number of topics which most appealed to
my students and hopefully will interest the wider public which
appreciates the importance of the law for the future of Europe
and indeed of the world. Some of the themes are essentially historical – such as the origin of the nineteenth-century German
Civil Code; some are also comparative – such as the contrast

between common law and civil law; others address present-day concerns – such as the interpretation of the Constitution of the United States (an outstanding example of legal scripture); and finally the future of European law is studied extensively and the question asked whether a truly common legal science is conceivable in a united twenty-first-century Europe, harking back to the days when the *ius commune* was the common science and language of lawyers from Aberdeen to Naples and from Cracow to Coimbra.

For the general background to these discussions the reader may turn to my *Historical introduction to private law* (Cambridge, 1992; repr. 1994) and my *Historical introduction to western constitutional law* (Cambridge, 1995).

Ghent, July 2001   R. C. VAN CAENEGEM

CHAPTER I

THE NATIONAL CODES: A TRANSIENT PHASE

ONE CODE FOR EVERY COUNTRY?

Present-day Europeans live under their national systems of law, which are almost invariably codified. Frenchmen live under the *Code civil*, Germans under the *Bürgerliches Gesetzbuch* and the English under their own uncodified common law. A few years ago the Dutch obtained a brand-new civil code, to replace that of 1838. European courts of justice, the European Commission, the European Parliament and European laws have not yet altered the basic fact that people live under national laws which were produced by the sovereign national states. And most people, no doubt, find this a natural state of affairs, as natural as their various languages. What they do not realize and would be surprised to find out, is that this 'natural state of affairs' is, on the time scale of European history, quite recent (going back only one or two centuries) and that the rise of the European Union may turn it into a brief and transient phase. That a future United Europe will strive for some degree of legal unification is plausible but, of course, uncertain. What is certain, however, is that medieval and early modern Europe managed without national legal systems. People lived either under local customs or under the two cosmopolitan, supranational systems – the law of the Church and the neo-Roman law of the universities (known as 'the common, written laws', or the learned *ius commune*). That every country should have its own strictly national law and be unaffected by others for many centuries was quite unthinkable. Cross-fertilization was the order of the day, because the law was seen as a vast treasure house from which kings and nations could pick and choose what suited them. We shall now present five illustrations of the transnational character of the law in Old Europe, the first three offering striking paradoxes.

ANGLO-NORMAN FEUDAL LAW

The first paradox is the continental origin of the English common law. To many people, who see the common law as quintessentially English, the realization of this historical fact comes as a shock. Yet, a fact it is. Nobody will deny that the common law has indeed developed in the course of the centuries into a peculiarly English phenomenon, that it has been instrumental in shaping the English character and is a great English achievement. Nevertheless at its very beginning it was the feudal law as administered by the English royal courts under King Henry II. That feudal law had been imported into England by the Norman conquerors and had basically been developed on the Continent, from the days of Charlemagne onwards. The law administered in the court of Henry II was Anglo-Norman, shared by the duchy of Normandy and the kingdom of England, and formed the legal basis of the landed wealth of the knightly class that ruled on both sides of the Channel under its common king-duke. Fiefs in England and Normandy were similar institutions and the English royal writs had their exact counterparts in the Norman ducal *briefs* (*brevia* was their common Latin name). Moreover, Henry II, who was the father of the English common law and took a great personal interest in legal problems, was a French prince who belonged to the ancient provincial dynasty of the counts of Anjou and ruled over a greater part of France (Anjou, Normandy and Aquitaine) than the king of France himself. His 'empire' was a conglomerate of national or provincial states, and it was only after the 'loss of Normandy' to France in 1204 that the kingdom and the duchy went their separate ways and the original Anglo-Norman law became purely English. It continued the work of Henry II in England, while Normandy came under the influence of Roman law (as did other parts of

France). Maitland's authoritative voice, 'The law which prevails in England at the end of the twelfth century, more especially the private law, is in a certain sense very French. It is a law evoked by French-speaking men, many of whom are of French race, many of whom have but begun to think of themselves as Englishmen; in many respects it is closely similar to that which prevailed in France', may be quoted here.[1]

GERMANIC ELEMENTS IN THE *CODE CIVIL*

My second illustration – and paradox – is that French law – and the *Code civil* of 1804 in particular – were deeply influenced by Germanic and feudal customary law. The Franks and other Germanic peoples who overran Gaul and settled on old Roman land, particularly in the north, brought with them their customary law, whose most famous monument is the Salic law (oldest version early sixth century). Whereas they gave up their tribal gods for Christianity and to a large extent gave up their language for vulgar Latin and proto-French, they stuck to their ancient laws. Consequently the northern two-thirds of France lived for centuries, not by the Roman as in ancient Gaul, but by Germanic customary law. It was only in the southern third of the kingdom that the former, in one form or another, survived. These two parts of France, which subsisted right up to the *Code civil*, are known respectively as *pays de droit coutumier* and *pays de droit écrit* (Roman law being bookish and written). Towards the end of the Middle Ages the monarchy ordered these old local and regional customs to be put in writing and published as law, so that these norms survived the impact of Roman law and deeply marked the *Code civil* itself. An important factor in this state of affairs was the Custom of Paris ('homologated' in the early sixteenth century) which became the cornerstone of

[1] Cambridge University Library, Add. Ms. 6987, fo. 124, quoted by J. Hudson, 'Maitland and Anglo-Norman law', 28 in J. Hudson (ed.), *The history of English law. Centenary essays on 'Pollock and Maitland'* (Oxford, 1996, Proceedings of the British Academy, 89).

an ideal general French law, and Paris was situated in the northern, customary part of France (the frontier between north and
south followed a line west to east not far south of the Loire).
The authors of the *Code civil* on the whole managed to establish
a reasonable synthesis of the two great traditions in their new
lawbook, obligations and contract being based on Roman, and
family and property on Germanic and feudal customary law.
But they could not always avoid heated arguments, as appeared
when the articles on the estate of married people were discussed:
the north was attached to the Germanic community of goods
and the south to the Roman dotal system (marriage settlement
in trust for the married woman): fiery patriotic southerners decried the community of goods as barbaric and stemming from
the primeval Germanic forests. The *Code* eventually adopted the
northern custom of the joint estate of husband and wife (administered by the husband) as the norm, but allowed the southerners
to choose the Roman system if they so wished.[2]

THE GERMAN CIVIL CODE BASED ON ROMAN LAW

Our third illustration is even more of a paradox, as it concerns
the Roman character of the German Civil Code of 1900. If the
Germanic customs survived so strongly in (northern) Gaul, they
should have totally prevailed in Germany, i.e. those lands east
of the Rhine and north of the Danube that stayed outside the
Roman empire. In other words, according to the rules of logic,
German civil law ought to be Germanic, just as French civil
law should have been Roman, France belonging to the Latin
world and being situated on ancient Roman soil. But history
does not always – or even usually – listen to the dictates of logic,
but follows its own, wayward paths. However strange it may

---

[2] J. Hilaire, *La Vie du droit. Coutumes et droit écrit* (Paris, 1994), 44; B. Beignier, 'Le chêne
et l'olivier' in *Ecrits en hommage à Jean Foyer* (Paris, 1997), 355–75. The nineteenth
century, in fact, witnessed the triumph of the *régime de la communauté* in the south, to
the detriment of the traditional dotal system. Normandy, although situated in the
north, also lived according to the latter. See J. Musset, *Les régimes des biens entre époux en
droit normand du XIVe siècle à la Révolution française* (Caen, 1997).

seem, it is an incontrovertible fact that the *Bürgerliches Gesetzbuch* is profoundly marked by Roman law, even though its language is German and its public the German citizenry. This surprising state of affairs can only be explained by the peculiar course of German political history – we refer of course, to the conscious decision taken at the end of the fifteenth century to 'receive' the Roman learned law of the medieval universities as the national law of Germany and to abandon the existing multitude of local and regional customs: a momentous step known as the *Rezeption*.

Emperor Maximilian and the humanists in his entourage dreamt of a modern German nation state, to replace the divided medieval kingdom. Germany had missed the boat of centralization and unification because of the involvement of her kings with the Roman empire and Italian politics, but this was going to change and the new German nation state would be provided, *inter alia*, with one national law, to replace the fragmented customs. This new law was to be, not the northern *Sachsenspiegel* or the southern *Schwabenspiegel*, but the learned Roman law of the medieval schools. Thus Germany would acquire in one fell swoop one common law (*gemeines Recht*) and the best Europe had on offer. As this was a legacy from imperial Rome and known as *Kaiserrecht*, it linked the German empire to the glories of Antiquity. The *Rezeption* was ordained by the German Estates and a new supreme court, the *Reichskammergericht* or Imperial Chamber Tribunal, was instituted in 1495 to implement and supervise this momentous 'legal transplant'. Half the judges were to be learned jurists, graduates in Roman law, and the other half knights, but by the middle of the sixteenth century they were all required to be holders of a law degree. From the sixteenth to the nineteenth century this 'received' foreign system was the basis of legal scholarship in Germany and its greatest triumph came in 1896 when the parliament of the German empire promulgated a civil code that was fundamentally Roman-based and professor-made (more about this in chapter 6). The decision of 1495 was all the more remarkable as medieval Germany had produced an imposing array of law books of her own and some of her *Schöffengerichte* or aldermen's courts, such as Magdeburg and Leipzig, had developed an extensive case law, which was authoritative in large areas, particularly in the east. Nevertheless this age-old, well-documented and established tradition was – largely but not completely – jettisoned at the end of the Middle Ages. 'Receptions' and 'legal transplants'[3] are not unknown in other places and at other times. One of the most striking examples in our own age was the adoption by Japan, at the time of the Meiji revolution, of the German Civil Code for the modern westernized Japanese empire. When the country decided to follow western examples, it first looked to England, which was the leading world power of the time, but the absence of an English civil code proved an insuperable obstacle. So the Japanese turned their attention to France, also a successful colonizing power of world stature and provided with a famous civil code. Preparations were made for the adoption of the Napoleonic lawbook and Professor Boissonnade went to Japan to prepare the way. Students at the old Paris Faculty of Law, near the Pantheon, are reminded of his efforts by a bust of the great jurist on the first floor, with two inscriptions, one reading *E. Boissonnade. Conseiller légiste accrédité du gouvernement japonais et professeur à l'Université Impériale de Tokio 1873–1895* and the other *Au Professeur E. Boissonnade Hommages des Japonais reconnaissants Paris 1934.* Politics and military events, however, upset these plans, as the French defeat at the hands of Bismarck in 1870 suggested to the Japanese – by some weird logic – that German might be superior to French law, as German weapons had beaten the French. Hence the Japanese decision to adopt the *Bürgerliches Gesetzbuch*, two years after its promulgation in Germany (modernization was clearly an urgent business in the land of the rising sun). So the sixth-century lawbook of Justinian first became the leading textbook of western medieval universities, four centuries later the law of modern Germany, after another four centuries the cornerstone of the civil code of

---

[3] The phrase is borrowed from A. Watson, *Legal transplants. An approach to comparative law* (2nd edn, Athens (Ga.), London, 1993).

the Wilhelmine Reich and – for the time being – ended its career as the law of twentieth-century Japan. It had travelled west, then east and then further east again, in a voyage that spanned the world.[4]

CHANGE OR CONTINUITY?

Some European countries, like Germany, have experienced abrupt changes in their legal development, whereas others have known great continuity; the phenomenon deserves some comments, under the heading 'old and new law in the European experience'. Indeed, some nations have made sharp and abrupt breaks with their past, which was rejected wholesale in order to make room for a radically new course; others witnessed a majestic, unperturbed continuity throughout many centuries with minor piecemeal adaptations, so that their legal experience is like a 'seamless web'. We shall now briefly discuss three cases: Germany, France and England.

Germany, as we have just seen, embarked on an entirely new venture around AD 1500 when it adopted Roman law. Respectable age-old customs, which had produced scholarly analysis and a considerable body of case law, were rejected and replaced by the *ius commune* of the universities. It is not easy for us to imagine what it meant when the aldermen of Frankfurt, solid and educated burghers but no Latin speakers, were told to forget about their familiar homespun law and to give judgement according to the *consilia* of Baldus and Bartolus! As they could not take a law degree in the Open University, the best they could do was to follow the advice of the town clerk, who had a law degree and could explain the merits of the case according to *Kaiserrecht* (they could also gain some elementary instruction

---

[4] Some recent work on the Japanese code: F. B. Verwaijen, 'Early reception of western legal thought in Japan 1841–1868' (Leiden, 1996, Doct. Diss.); Ishii Shiro, 'The reception of the occidental systems by the Japanese legal system', in M. Doucet and J. Vanderlinden (eds.), *La Réception des systèmes juridiques: implantation et destin. Textes . . . colloque . . . 1992* (Brussels, 1994), 239–66.

from the *vocabularia iuris* that were being printed around that time). The scene will remind some English readers of the magistrates' court, where the clerk is at hand with technical advice (and has the authoritative reference works at his fingertips) for the magistrates who have never seen the inside of a Law School.[5] We would, however, like to sound a cautionary note, for the break with the past was not as absolute as the official German policy envisaged. Indeed, the old native tradition survived in various ways and there was resistance to the new-fangled constitutions and rescripts. This was especially the case in Saxony, where the memory of the *Sachsenspiegel* was never lost: even in the nineteenth century, when *Pandektenrecht* (the Roman law as developed by German professors on the basis of Justinian's Digest or Pandects) was at its height, commentaries on the Mirror of the Saxons were still influential[6] and the kingdom of Saxony even had a civil code of its own.[7] In the eighteenth century the study of German history had initiated a renewed interest in the old legal lore and a romantic reappraisal of Germanic Antiquity and the German Middle Ages (we shall later refer to the two nineteenth-century Schools of the Germanists and the Romanists that were the result).

France witnessed a similar break with the past at the time of the Revolution. Previously, and right up to the seventeenth century, people had thought that 'old law was good law', but the Enlightenment and belief in progress had changed all that, and old law became synonymous with bad law which had to be abolished. This the Revolution proceeded to do. Ancient laws and the

---

[5] See the graphic description in the classic H. Coing, *Die Rezeption des römischen Rechts in Frankfurt am Main. Ein Beitrag zur Rezeptionsgeschichte* (Frankfurt, 1939).

[6] The medieval *Sachsenspiegel* and its later versions and commentaries were considered a subsidiary source of the law, called the *gemeines Sachsenrecht* throughout the nineteenth century. See H. Schlosser, F. Sturm and H. Weber, *Die rechtsgeschichtliche Exegese. Römisches Recht, Deutsches Recht, Kirchenrecht* (2nd edn, Munich, 1993), 94.

[7] The *Bürgerliches Gesetzbuch für das Königreich Sachsen* was the last great European codification before the German Code of 1896/1900. It was promulgated in 1863 and replaced in general by the pan-German Code. It was based on the learned *Gemeine Recht*, combined with traditional Saxon material. It was generally considered an outstanding text and led to considerable commentaries and authoritative judgements.

ancient constitution disappeared and, after a period of unsuccessful attempts at codifying new law, Napoleon managed to publish various codes for the whole of France, the most important being the Civil Code of 1804. They had a lasting impact and are fundamental in many ways till this day. The Napoleonic codes not only introduced new law, but expressly abrogated all old laws, customs, ordinances and so on which had formed the multicoloured mosaic of the old legal landscape: a monolithic system was erected in its place. Hence the well-known divide of French law into the pre-revolutionary *ancien droit* and the Napoleonic *droit nouveau* (the intervening fifteen years being known as the *droit intermédiaire*). Until this day teaching in the French Law Faculties concerns either 'the law', i.e. the law of the codes, or 'legal history', i.e. the study of the *ancien droit*, the former being concerned with living law and the latter with museum pieces. One is either a lawyer or a legal historian and contact between the two disciplines is minimal. Yet, here again the situation is not as clear cut as would seem at first sight. The Civil Code was in reality far from containing only 'new law', as it had taken over a considerable mass of customary material, especially from the *Coutume de Paris*, and incorporated, often verbatim, the writings of eighteenth-century jurists, such as Robert-Joseph Pothier (*d.* 1772), who had taught at the university of Orleans and was familiar with both Roman and customary law. The Civil Code was the product of a post-revolutionary era and was deeply conservative, particularly as far as respect for property and family values and the leading role of the father and husband were concerned. Nevertheless certain revolutionary achievements, such as legal equality, divorce and the abolition of serfdom, were maintained. The most conservative of Napoleon's codes was the Code of Civil Procedure, which repeated verbatim large parts of the *Ordonnance civile pour la réformation de la justice* of Louis XIV. And although Roman law was abolished, together with all other sources of the Ancien Régime, nineteenth-century judges had no qualms in referring to it in their judgements and betraying a thorough acquaintance with the law of Justinian, which continued to be taught at the universities.[8]

In contrast to the German and French experience, English legal history is the ideal type of traditionalism and uninterrupted continuity. There is no 'old common law' or 'new common law', just one ageless common law, based on the wisdom of centuries. Its course is marked by adaptation, not by change of what is in any case immutable. Even the reforms of the nineteenth century have not basically altered the ancient, uncodified common law, in spite of changes in procedure and judicial organization. Cases are quoted that go back to Sir William Blackstone (*d.* 1780) and that universal treasure house of the common law, Sir Edward Coke (*d.* 1634), who himself sometimes harked back to precedents in Littleton (*d.* 1481) and even the great Henry de Bracton (*d.* 1268), author of a massive, lonely Treatise on the Laws and Customs of the Realm of England. Death sentences were still being pronounced in the twentieth century on the strength of medieval statutes without any reservation about their antiquity. Sir Roger Casement, for example, a British subject and an Irish nationalist, who tried to raise an army in Germany against Britain, was hanged in London in 1916 on the strength of the Statute of Treasons of 1352. However, not even English lawyers go back to Queen Boadicea: there are limits, and the official 'limit of legal memory' is the date of the coronation of King Richard I on 3 September 1189, beyond which the courts do not go back. That date was fixed by the Statute of Westminster I (AD 1275) on the limitation for writs of right and the Statutes of *quo warranto* of 1289–90, probably because it was conceivable that a living man had been told by his father what he had seen in 1189, and in a proprietary action for land the demandant's champion was allowed to speak of what his father

---

[8] See the detailed survey in H. Kooiker, 'Lex scripta abrogata. De derde Renaissance van het Romeinse recht. Een onderzoek naar de doorwerking van het oude recht na de invoering van civielrechtelijke codificaties in het begin van de negentiende eeuw, I: De uitwendige ontwikkeling' (Nijmegen, 1996, Doct. Diss.). Concerns France and The Netherlands.

had seen.[9] Most legal textbooks in England start with a List of
Cases and a List of Statutes, both going back several centuries
and without any visible caesura.

The most comprehensive, encyclopaedic history of English
law was undertaken by Sir William Searle Holdsworth (*d.* 1944),
an Oxford professor and fellow of All Souls College.[10] He per-
sonifies the belief in and love of the continuity of English law:
real change never occurred, only adaptation of ancient principles. He reminds the reader of the medieval horror of *novitates*,
innovations. He also embodied the traditional reverence for the
Bench and belief in the pre-eminence of judges as the 'makers
of the law'[11] and the concomitant aversion to the legislator as
an agent of legal development. One trait of the conservatism of
the Bench is attachment to precedents: 'what was good in the
past must be good in our own time' is by definition a conservative attitude. *Stare decisis* is a weighty common-law principle,
even though it is not universally held and is not as ancient as is
sometimes thought. There were judges in the past who maintained that they had sworn to uphold justice and not to uphold
precedent, and therefore felt free to ignore existing case law,
and there are famous judges in our own time – such as Lord
Denning[12] – who dare to ignore precedent for the sake of justice; moreover the strict doctrine of *stare decisis* first emerged in
the later nineteenth century.[13] Nor is traditionalism to be found

---

9 F. Pollock and F. W. Maitland, *The history of English law before the time of Edward I*,
   I (2nd edn, Cambridge, 1968), 168.
10 We refer, of course, to his *History of English law* (London, 1903–72, 17 vols., several
   posth.).
11 See his *Some makers of English Law* (Cambridge, 1938), Tagore lectures 1937–8.
12 Alfred Thompson Denning, who was created a Life Peer of 1957, was born in 1900.
   He studied mathematics and law at Oxford, was a Lord Justice of Appeal from 1948
   to 1957, a Lord of Appeal in Ordinary from 1957 to 1962 and Master of the Rolls
   from 1962 to 1982. See on him: C. M. Schmitthoff, 'Lord Denning and the contemporary scene. A homage . . .', *Journal of Business Law* (1979), 97–104; R. Stevens, *Law
   and politics. The House of Lords as a judicial body, 1800–1976* (London, 1979), 488–505;
   E. Heward, *Lord Denning* (2nd edn, Chichester, 1997).
13 See H. J. Berman and C. J. Reid Jr., 'The transformation of English legal science:
   from Hale to Blackstone', *Emory Law Journal* 45 (1996), 448. The authors quote
   Chief Justice Vaughan of the Court of Common Pleas as saying in 1673: 'If a judge

in legal circles only. The English ecclesiastical establishment also prefers continuity to change and some people, being unable 'to eliminate the Reformation altogether', liked to see that cataclysmic break with the past as 'a small and predictable shudder in a general march of continuity'.[14] But, here again, things are not so absolute as they might seem. We should not be befogged by the *laudatores temporis acti*, for a critical look at the past will soon show that there was a good deal of real and important change: the majestic flow of English legal history was on several occasions diverted or interrupted. The Puritan Revolution undertook a drastic overhaul of the common law and its courts. It wanted to introduce a register of land-holding – comparable to the later *Grundbuch* in Germany – and to codify the law, and it installed the Hale Commission for that purpose, so named after its Chairman, the learned Sir Matthew Hale (*d.* 1676). It replaced the archaic and impenetrable Law French by the English language in the courts and generally attempted modernization and democratization. That the Restoration in 1660 reversed or stopped these endeavours does not make them less interesting (even though traditional legal histories tend to skate over them as being just a brief interlude). The urge to innovate arose again and in full force in the nineteenth century, when the writ system, created in the twelfth century, was abolished and the fusion of common law and equity was brought about, two ancient bodies of law with their distinct courts and rules of procedure. Also the Judicature Acts of 1873 and 1875 created a modern system of law courts. Yet, in spite of all this reforming zeal, the substance of the common law was admittedly saved: the impact of the judges on the law remained very strong (about which more in chapter 3) and, above all, English law avoided codification. Also, although common law and equity were, as we have seen, fused and there were no separate common law courts and a court of chancery,

---

conceives a judgement given in another Court to be erroneous, he being sworn to judge according to law, that is, in his conscience, ought not to give the like judgement...' See *Ibid.*, 449 for the emergence of *stare decisis* in the later nineteenth century.
[14] G. R. Elton, *F. W. Maitland* (London, 1985), 72.

nevertheless the age-old distinction survives till this day in the Chancery Division and the Queen's Bench Division of the High Court. And to everyone's surprise the House of Lords' jurisdiction in appeal survived the Judicature Acts and the creation of a Court of Appeal, so that England has two courts of appeal one above the other, and not one court of appeal capped by one Court of Cassation, as a continental lawyer would expect.

THE *IUS COMMUNE*, TRANSNATIONAL BY DEFINITION

The supranational law *par excellence* was, of course, the *ius commune*. This is not a paradox but self evident, as it was the learned system produced by the European universities and common to all Latin Christendom. Based on the study of the great lawbooks of Emperor Justinian (*d.* 565), in which the wisdom of the Roman jurists and the imperial administrators was recorded for all time, it became known as the *Corpus iuris civilis*. Promulgated as law in the eastern Roman empire after the west had been overrun by the Germanic peoples, it only surfaced in Italy in the late eleventh century. It became the basis of commentaries and teaching, first in Bologna and then in numerous other universities. As the *Corpus* was in Latin, so were the later commentaries, textbooks, teaching and disputations. As Latin was the spoken and written language of scholars all over western Europe, this reborn or neo-Roman law became the common law of all jurists without the interference of any national boundaries. Around the same time and in the same university of Bologna the systematic study of canon or ecclesiastical law was started, in which development Roman law played a fundamental role: the science of canon law was impossible without a basis of Roman law. Although Roman law and canon law remained two distinct disciplines, with their own Faculties, they were so closely linked that they are often referred to as the 'common learned – or written – laws' and they constitute the two parts of the *ius commune*. The symbiosis of both legal systems was facilitated by the fact that the Church was supposed to live by Roman law (*ecclesia vivit lege Romana*), and that ever since the Gregorian reform the centralized organization of the Church came to look more and more like that of imperial Rome and that the great sixth-century compilation – containing much of the jurisprudence of heathen Rome – was published by a great Christian emperor.

The term 'common law' (*ius commune, droit commun, gemeines Recht*) is used in so many senses and contexts that a word of explanation may be appropriate. The English 'common law' is so called because it was common to all of England, in contrast to local customs. The *ius commune* is so called because it was common to all scholars. *Gemeines Recht* was the name given in Germany after the *Rezeption* to the common learned law of Germany, based on the *ius commune*. In French *droit commun* is sometimes used in contrast to the political sphere (as in *crimes de droit commun* as against treasonable wrongdoing) but there was also a *droit commun français*, created by the endeavours of Ancien Régime scholars who hoped to establish a legal system common to all of France, overarching the existing regional diversities.

Canon law shared with Roman law its learned, systematic character; both were based on written texts and the object of teaching and scholarly classification. However, before the twelfth century canon law was just a set of norms that ruled everyday life and were based on a multitude of canons of Church councils and papal decretals issued in the course of a millennium. Canon law started as applied law and later developed into a scholarly system: it was a set of rules before it became a science. The Roman law of the schools, by contrast, started as a science and eventually entered everyday practice and became applied law.

Medieval canon law was the first common law of the whole of western Europe, as it was administered, taught and studied in the whole of Latin Christendom without any regard for political, ethnic or linguistic frontiers. Even after the Reformation had disrupted this old unity, the law of the medieval Church went on to dominate ecclesiastical organization and the lives of ordinary people – especially in matrimonial matters – even in

Protestant countries. In the case of England the result of Reformation and Counter-Reformation went even further, as the modern law of the Anglican Church contains medieval elements that were eliminated in the Catholic Church by the Council of Trent (which had no authority in England). Medieval canon law was applied by separate ecclesiastical courts, competent *ratione personae* – for clerics – and *ratione materiae* – mainly in questions of sexual morality (which concerns a very important segment of personal and social behaviour). Church courts were, of course, also competent for questions of orthodoxy and heresy – the ideological debate, in modern parlance – so that their impact on the beliefs and the way of life of the people at large was immense, all the more so since their judgements were enforced by the state, the 'secular arm' of the Church. These courts were also the places where ordinary people came in contact with the learned law and the learned forms of process, developed by Romanists and canonists from the twelfth century onwards and therefore known as Roman-canonical procedure. For most medieval people, who never approached a university or read a book in their lives, the Church courts in their everyday activity were the only places where they came in direct contact with the *ius commune*.

At a time when many people talk about a possible, future European state, it is noteworthy that the first experiment in that line was the medieval Church, which was a quasi-state and comprised the nations of the present European Union.[15] It was a vast, self-sufficient, self-contained and efficient organization, extending over a very large area (from Ireland to the Holy Land, and from Sweden to Portugal) containing numerous nations, languages and cultures. Like the state, the Church had its own rules, organized its own dispute settlement and disposed of its own security arrangements – with its own organs for criminal prosecution and its own prisons. Its financial organization,

---

[15] We are, of course, not talking here of the papal territory in the centre of Italy, which was a true state with the same attributes of temporal power as so many other regional political formations in feudal times.

supported by the supranational Italian banking companies, was a model of efficiency, whereas its fiscal inventiveness for tapping new sources of revenue might be a source of inspiration to present-day ministers of finance (let us hope that not too many of them study the system of papal benefices). The Church lived under a centralized hierarchy, strictly organized from country parishes up to the Roman *curia*. It had one central government, with many departments, and it had a parliament, the ecumenical council, where representatives from many countries and walks of life met, deliberated and made laws. The power and the role of these Church councils have varied enormously – as is the case with parliaments in modern states – but there have been moments when they seriously attempted to wrest control of the Church from the papal government, and their composition was so international and so comprehensive – containing laymen as well as secular and regular clergy – that they can truly be described as the forerunners and prefigurations of the present-day European parliament (particularly since they discussed a wide variety of topics, by no means all ecclesiastical). I am referring, of course, to the great councils of Pisa, Constance, Basel and Florence in what is known as the Conciliar Epoch (late fourteenth and first half of the fifteenth century).[16]

However, for a variety of reasons the medieval Church was not really a state. It had no army, for though the Crusades mobilized by the papacy could be considered a sort of papal task force, they certainly were no standing army. The Church had no citizenship and no fixed territory but, above all, its *raison d'être* was different. Its aim was to guide the faithful to salvation, whereas the state was expected to ensure the external and internal safety of its citizens (even though some modern states think that they have to look after the happiness and wellbeing of their citizens as well). In some ways the medieval Church was like modern multinationals,

---

[16] See B. Tierney, *Foundations of the conciliar theory* (Cambridge, 1955); M. J. Wilks, *The problem of sovereignty in the later Middle Ages* (Cambridge, 1963); and the survey in H. Jedin (ed.), *Handbuch der Kirchengeschichte*, III: *Die mittelalterliche Kirche*, 2. *Halbband* (Freiburg, 1968), 490–588 (by E. Iserloh).

which also have their own hierarchy, vast budgets, no citizenship, but internal security arrangements (and even external defence mechanisms against hostile take-over bids).

Medieval Roman law keeps surprising every historian. Indeed, here was a West-European system of law, based on a compilation made some six centuries earlier in a foreign empire. Justinian, Institutes, Digest, Code and Novels belonged to the classical world, which was utterly different from feudal and agrarian Europe of AD 1100; the Digest, the most inspiring part, was even the work of pagan authors. The Roman empire, where the *Corpus* originated, was a mere memory among the emerging nation states of the twelfth century. Moreover, Justinian's lawbook, which attracted so much passionate attention, had no legal authority in the West at all. It had never been promulgated there, either by an ancient east-Roman emperor or by a medieval German king–Roman emperor (that changed only with the German *Rezeption* around AD 1500). Legally speaking the *Corpus* had as much binding force in twelfth-century Europe as the Assyrian clay tablets in their cuneiform script have today. And yet the great book and the vast superstructure of lectures and treatises built upon it acquired an authority of their own and became the cornerstone of the modern civil law that, together with the English common law, dominates our own world.

One of the attractions of that neo-Roman law was its cosmopolitanism, as it was similarly taught, using the same textbooks and in the same Latin language, in all western universities, where professors and students from every country congregated (we shall see in chapter 5 what caused this remarkable phenomenon).

At first the study of the *Corpus*, in the form of literal explanations ('glossing'), was a mere academic exercise, but soon the Schools began to take notice of the real medieval world, as the real world took notice of them, and neo-Roman reasoning and categories were applied even to feudal institutions – although the feudal system was undreamt of in the world of Ulpian and Modestinus. Roman law began to influence the courts, first the ecclesiastical and then the secular, and so affected the social fabric in general.

Let us look at one example among many, to show how the law of Bologna was quoted as authority (*imperio rationis* if not *ratione imperii*)[17] in the discussion of a purely feudal, typically medieval problem and how customary law became mixed up with Justinian-inspired learning. Feudalism was based on the personal loyalty of the vassal to the lord, to whom he had sworn an oath of fealty. The vassal was expected to stand by his lord, who had provided him with a fief, in all circumstances and against all his enemies. At the top of the feudal pyramid stood the king, who was at the same time the highest feudal overlord and a monarch by God's grace (hence the term 'the feudal monarchy'). So the – very feudal – question arose whether a vassal had to stand by a lord who rebelled against the king. In terms of personal loyalty the answer was positive, but in terms of monarchic theory the answer was negative. So which was the top priority, the loyalty to one's lord or obedience to the head of state? Jean de Blanot, a civilian who died probably shortly after 1281, addressed this much debated question with arguments from Roman law. Admitting that there are arguments for the idea that, on the strength of his personal oath of fealty, a vassal is obliged to support his lord against the latter's lord, even if he happens to be the king, Jean de Blanot maintains the contrary 'because a baron who rises against the king violates the *lex Julia maiestatis*, since it would be like machinating the death of a magistrate of the Roman people; he would act against the emperor (*princeps*), as the king of France is an emperor (*princeps*) in his kingdom'.[18] So in order to protect the monarchic principle against what some considered feudal

---

[17] 'At the command of reason and not because of the authority of the empire.'

[18] Text and commentary in M. Boulet-Sautel, 'Jean de Blanot et la conception du pouvoir royal au temps de Louis IX', in *Septième centenaire de la mort de Saint Louis. Actes des Colloques de Royaumont et de Paris (1970)* (Paris, 1976), 57–68. See also R. Feenstra, 'Jean de Blanot et la formule "Rex Franciae in regno suo princeps est"', in *Etudes d'histoire du droit canonique dédiées à Gabriel Le Bras*, II (Paris, 1965), 885–95. See Digest, Book XLVIII, Title 4 'ad legem Juliam maiestatis'; Engl. transl. in S. P. Scott (transl.), *The civil law*, IX (Cincinnati, 1932), 25–28.

anarchy, Jean de Blanot invoked a law from Roman Antiquity on the protection of imperial majesty (and preserved in the Digest of Justinian) and assumed that this ancient *lex* overruled the feudal principle of his own time. He made his step even more daring by the fiction that the king of France was an emperor, which he clearly was not. In fact this was no more than a form of words to express the plausible notion that the king of France was the sovereign monarch of a sovereign country, who occupied in his kingdom the position the Roman *princeps* occupied in his empire. At first the writings of Jean de Blanot and his colleagues were scholarly exercises from the halls of the Schools, but soon they were quoted in court rooms and in the great political councils, and so Roman law began to conquer much of Europe.

Whether this learned *ius commune* could, in the twenty-first century, play a role in the elaboration of a common European science of private law is a question that naturally arises from the study of the past (and which we shall address in chapter 2).

THE ENGLISH COMMON LAW PURELY ENGLISH?

Having argued for the transnational character of the law in medieval and early modern Europe, I must now face the objection that there is one obvious exception. Surely, the critics will say, England is the great exception, since here we have a strictly national system of law that, except for a brief period at the very beginning, is quintessentially English, administered by English courts, developed by English judges, kings and parliaments and recorded in typical English Year Books, law reports and treatises. It even used its own cryptic and increasingly archaic language, called Law French, that was understood by a dwindling minority in England and diverged more and more from the French spoken on the Continent. All this is basically true and nobody denies that from the thirteenth century onwards the English common law was a truly national system, that was eventually exported by English people who settled in remote continents: English law was neither local nor cosmopolitan, it was national and it was

English (not Scottish, Welsh or Irish): it was the law of one particular nation state, one of the earliest and most enduring on the European scene.

Yet, here again, the true picture is less absolute than a first contact would make us believe. Indeed, English law also underwent the main international currents that swept all over Europe, as we shall try to demonstrate. Thus it is important to realize that the common law is not the only legal system known and followed in England. Indeed, English ecclesiastical courts applied the canon law of the Latin Church, even though customary variations were observed in the English Church as in many others. The old controversy between the Oxford medievalist and bishop, William Stubbs, and the Cambridge legal historian Frederic William Maitland was laid to rest long ago in favour of the latter, who rejected Stubbs' thesis that medieval England had applied its own national ecclesiastical law.[19] Moreover, the Court of Chancery, which originated in the fourteenth century and developed an important jurisdiction of its own, did not apply the common law, but produced its own equity, which in course of time became a distinct body of law, and followed its own rules of procedure, which were closer to the Roman-canonical than the common-law model.[20] The Court of Admiralty also followed a course of its own and applied the European *ius commune*, as was natural because of its concern with international shipping on the high seas.[21] Also Roman and canon law were taught at Oxford and Cambridge where future diplomats and bishops

---

[19] Elton, *F. W. Maitland*, 69–79. The occasion for Maitland's research was the 1883 report of a Royal Commission of which Stubbs was a member, which declared that 'the canon law of Rome, though always regarded as of great authority in England, was not held to be binding on the courts' in the Middle Ages (a conclusion supported by Stubbs in a long *Historical appendix*). Maitland's thesis can be found in his *Roman canon law in the Church of England* (London, 1898). The problem, far from being merely historical and academic, touched upon some raw political and religious nerves.

[20] The most fundamental study of the Court of Chancery in recent years can be found in the *Introduction* in D. E. C. Yale (ed.), *Lord Nottingham's Chancery cases* (London, 1961, Selden Soc. Publ., 79), 7–207.

[21] See the recent fundamental work of M. J. Prichard and D. E. C. Yale (eds.), *Hale and Fleetwood on Admiralty jurisdiction* (London, 1993, Selden Soc. Publ., 108), especially the 250-page Introduction. Sir Julius Caesar, whose career has been analysed extensively

were trained in the *ius commune*. Nor was the common law itself immune from Justinian's influence: its main doctrinal work in medieval times, the aforementioned Bracton's Treatise on the Laws and Customs of the Realm of England, is deeply marked by civilian learning, especially Azo's *Summa codicis*.[22] The great common lawyers of modern times, such as Hale and Blackstone, were well aware of continental jurisprudence and so were leading judges in the nineteenth century. Whether this justifies calling English law European[23] is a moot point, but it can certainly not be said that English law developed in splendid isolation.[24]

in recent times, sat as a judge in the London Court of Admiralty from 1582 to 1606. See L. M. Hill, *Bench and bureaucracy. The public career of Sir Julius Caesar, 1580–1606* (Cambridge, 1988); A. Wijffels, 'Sir Julius Caesar's notes on Admiralty cases: An alternative to law reporting?' in C. Stebbings (ed.), *Law reporting in England* (London, Rio Grande, 1995), 89–112; A. Wijffels, 'Julius Caesar's notes on POWS', *Legal History Review* 65 (1997), 349–72.

[22] The bibliography on Bracton is large. See for some recent assessments J. L. Barton, 'The mystery of Bracton', *Journal of Legal History* 14 (1993), no. 3, special issue, 1–142; H. H. Jakobs, *De similibus ad similia bei Bracton und Azo* (Frankfurt, 1996, Ius Commune Sonderhefte, 87).

[23] So R. Zimmermann, 'Der europäische Character des englischen Rechts. Historische Verbindungen zwischen civil law und common law', *Zeitschrift für Europäisches Recht* (1993), 4–51.

[24] We shall come back to the differences between common and civil law in chapter 3.

CHAPTER 2

IUS COMMUNE: THE FIRST UNIFICATION OF EUROPEAN LAW

TRIBES AND NATION STATES

In present-day Europe the basic nineteenth-century situation still prevails. On the Continent the codes have survived and the nation states are still going strong: 'one nation, one state, one code of law' describes it well enough. The same can be said of the uncodified English common law, whose hold on the country is still powerful. Law students of my generation, who had never heard of a European Commission, a European Parliament or European courts in Luxemburg and Strasbourg, took these monolithic national systems for granted. The most striking example could be found in the over-centralized France of the nineteenth century. Private law was based on one civil code and one code of civil procedure, which had formally replaced all previous norms and were valid for the whole territory. There was one tightly controlled network of Law Faculties where the one *Code civil* was taught under the supervision of one Ministry of Education. There was one Department of Justice to supervise the workings of the courts and one Court of Cassation, in Paris of course, to ensure the application of the one code and the uniformity of its interpretation. There was one body of jurisprudence, with a limited number of eminent professors who wrote authoritative treatises (sometimes called 'elementary' in spite of their containing numerous volumes) and all belonged to the one *Ecole de l'Exégèse* (on which more in chapter 4). The system was closed in the sense that no appeal to higher courts outside France was possible: the citizens were imprisoned in their 'sovereign' nation state, with their own laws and their own judges.

The contrast with previous centuries could not be greater, for Old Europe had known a legal fragmentation that we can hardly conceive. Europeans had lived under various Germanic tribal laws, attached not to a territory, but to men and women of common descent. When more settled conditions prevailed, people lived according to local customs, applied in numerous regions of various sizes. As kingdoms and principalities developed their political institutions, legislation gained some importance, either at a national, a regional or a local level (for certain towns or groups of villages). From the twelfth century onwards urban autonomy was an important factor and so were urban privileges and legislation. Long before that date feudal law had taken shape, with a set of norms of its own and valid for limited social groups and particular plots of land. The innumerable medieval corporations – universities, guilds and crafts – had their own laws and rules, and above it all the Church applied its canons and decretals and the neo-Roman law of the glossators and the commentators. All these laws were applied in different courts, which were sometimes competent for tiny plots of land or small quarters of a town. The fragmentation was so extreme that within a single agglomeration, neighbouring areas, districts and even buildings could fall under different legal systems and belong to different courts of aldermen, guilds, feudatories, lords, rural deans or hundreds. The amazing thing is that society coped so well with this miraculous multiplication of laws and courts. Demarcation disputes were frequent, but were usually solved peacefully: it took a Thomas Becket to turn a conflict on jurisdiction into a great and bloody political drama. Also, the multitude of urban laws led in fourteenth-century Italy to the rise, under the aegis of Bartolus, of a doctrine of the conflict of laws, i.e. international private law.

In the last analysis this legal – and political – state of affairs was the consequence of the all-pervading medieval diffusion of power, which had radically replaced the fundamental Roman notion of its absolute concentration. In Antiquity all legitimate authority derived from the emperor, even in the most remote provinces. The Middle Ages knew and accepted a multitude of autonomous sources of legitimate power, dispersed over a wide variety of persons and bodies.

THE MEDIEVAL *IUS COMMUNE*

Nevertheless, even in medieval times, some unifying forces were at work. The Church, as we have seen, comprehended all of western Christendom in one centralized organization, but its law had only a limited impact *ratione materiae* and *ratione personae*. The other half of the *ius commune*, Roman law, was initially cultivated only by a small elite of scholars, but eventually their teaching entered the practice of the courts and influenced the royal legislators and even the drafters of the homologated customs. In this sense medieval Roman law as a pan-European science was a unifying force.[1] The learned commentators of customary law, who had been trained as Roman lawyers, tended to apply the scholarly methods they had acquired at the university. This was the case, for example, when Charles Dumoulin wrote his commentaries on the Custom of Paris.[2] Moreover, kings who caused customary laws to be recorded and made them binding tended to give Roman law a supplementary role, in order to remedy the deficiencies and gaps in recorded customs.[3] Here again Roman law was a unifying force.

It would, however, be wrong to accept this traditional – and basically correct – interpretation without qualification. Indeed, in some quirky way Roman law also exerted a divisive influence

[1] For a recent very readable survey see the following volume of collected studies: E. J. H. Schrage, Non quia romanum sed quia ius. *Das Entstehen eines europäischen Rechtsbewusstseins im Mittelalter* (Goldbach, 1996, Bibliotheca Eruditorum, 17).

[2] They were based on the *Coutume de Paris* of 1510 and were so influential that when the *Coutume* was 'reformed' in 1580, his critical observations were the main source of the modifications and corrections in this new version. See J.-L. Thireau, *Charles du Moulin (1500–1566). Etudes sur les sources, la méthode, les idées politiques et économiques d'un juriste de la Renaissance* (Geneva, 1980, Travaux d'Humanisme et Renaissance, 176).

[3] See: J. Gilissen, 'Le Problème des lacunes du droit dans l'évolution du droit médiéval et moderne', in C. Perelman (ed.), *Le Problème des lacunes en droit* (Brussels, 1968), 197–246; J. Gilissen, *Introduction historique au droit* (Brussels, 1979), 332–3.

(in the sense of leading to diversity and not of causing conflict). It was divisive because its impact varied greatly from country to country and consequently created differences between them. If they had all 'received' the *ius commune* around the same time and with the same intensity, its unifying role would have been total, but this was not the case. Indeed, the impact of Roman law varied from close to nil (in the case of the English common law) to massive (in the case of the German Pandectists of the nineteenth century), with various shades in between: the seventeenth-century Roman Dutch law was built on a peculiar symbiosis of customary and learned law, and produced by the creative mind of Hugo Grotius (*d.* 1645). The ambivalent role of Roman law in medieval Europe was highlighted recently in a large and original book by an Italian scholar, Maurizio Lupoi,[4] who maintains that until the twelfth century Europe lived under a common Germanic-feudal law and that it was the progress of neo-Roman law which caused the great divide between common-law and civil-law countries and between the lands of the *Code civil* and those of the *Bürgerliches Gesetzbuch*. The common law, in this perspective, continued the un-Roman law of early medieval Europe, whereas the Continent took a different road and diverged (dare we say deviated?) from the common old stock (the Continent cut off from England instead of the other way around!). Certainly in the perspective of universal legal history, a system built on customs and case law must be judged more 'normal' than one produced by a quasi-theological exegesis of an ancient sacred text (more on this in chapter 4). Lupoi's thesis is refreshing and somewhat provocative, but deserves closer scrutiny. The archaic law of early medieval Europe admittedly presented a great similarity in its basic assumptions and attitudes – in its system of proofs, for example[5] – but the fact remains that there

---

[4] M. Lupoi, *Alle radici del mondo giuridico europeo. Saggio storico-comparativo* (Rome, 1994).
[5] See R. C. Van Caenegem, 'Methods of proof in western medieval law', in R. C. Van Caenegem, *Legal history: A European perspective* (London, Rio Grande, 1991), 71–113; R. C. Van Caenegem, 'Reflexions on rational and irrational modes of proof in medieval Europe', *Legal History Review* 58 (1990), 263–79.

was a noticeable difference between allodial and feudal lands, between urban and rural usages and privileges, and between the edicts and customs in various realms, countries and smaller districts. This diversity was being overcome by the new cosmopolitan learning. The question therefore arises whether a common European theory of private law – a new *ius commune* – could, in a united Europe, play the same unifying role as the old did between the twelfth and the eighteenth centuries.

TOWARDS A 'NEW *IUS COMMUNE*'?

Before presenting the debate that is raging nowadays on this point, a few preliminary remarks may be appropriate. In general terms a common doctrine, leading perhaps to a common law, should not be too difficult to achieve. We refer, without entering into details, to advanced efforts and projects that have already been realized in specific fields in the countries of the civil law[6] and we remind the reader of the fundamental unity of, *inter alia,* the law of obligations, which is based on Roman law throughout the Continent.

The great stumbling block is, of course, the un-Roman and uncodified English common law. Here learned opinion is divided between the optimists, who maintain that England is not as insular as is generally believed, and the pessimists, who are convinced that the gulf between common law and civil law is unbridgeable.

---

[6] We refer to Ole Lando's *Principles of European contract law* (1995) and the (wider) *Unidroit principles for international commercial contracts* (1994–5). We also refer to several European casebooks, based on the judgments of the Court in Luxemburg, that are being prepared by, *inter alia*, the above-mentioned W. Van Gerven. We especially draw attention to the *Draft rules on civil procedure* of the Storme Working Group. See M. Storme (ed.), *Rapprochement du droit judiciaire de l'Union européenne. Approximation of judiciary law in the European Union* (Dordrecht, Boston, London, 1994). This volume contains the proposals of the Commission for a European law of civil procedure, founded in 1984 under Storme's chairmanship. The results were put before the European Commission in 1993 (see H. Roth's critical considerations in *Zeitschrift für Europäisches Privatrecht* (1997), 567–72). The reader will be aware of two resolutions, of 1989 and 1994, in favour of the unification of European private law passed by the European Parliament.

Let us begin with the optimists. They opened the debate with a bang when, in 1992, B. De Witte and C. Forder edited, under the auspices of the Faculty of Law in the University of Maastricht – a town that was to become famous in the history of European unification – a stout volume entitled *The common law of Europe and the future of legal education. Le Droit commun de l'Europe et l'avenir de l'enseignement juridique.*[6a] The general tone of the volume was set by the title of T. Koopmans's article: 'Towards a new *"ius commune"*', (43–51) and as the coming of this European law was taken more or less for granted, it was normal that the question be posed about how the teaching of this new legal system was organized in various parts of present-day Europe and America and how it was to be conceived in the future.[7] In the same year P. Ulmer examined the question of a possible transition 'from a German to a European private law', presented a balanced evaluation of the possibilities and thoroughly discussed the role of the Law Faculties on the road to a European private law, through research and teaching.[8] But it was in 1993 that the great debate on the 'English stumbling block' was opened with an article by the aforementioned R. Zimmermann under the resounding title 'The European character of English law'.[9] The subtitle 'Historical links between civil law and common law' somewhat mitigated the first shock felt by many readers, who knew that English lawyers had, indeed, followed continental developments with interest, but were doubtful whether this had given English

---

[6a] Deventer, 1992.

[7] See, for example, C. Flinterman, *European legal education in the future: Some concluding observations* (113–18); R. De Groot, *European legal education in the 21st century* (7–30); K. Lipstein, *European legal education in the future: Teaching the 'common law of Europe'* (255–63); G. Van den Bergh, Ius commune, *a history with a future* (593–608). This last author tries to convince European jurists 'that it is worth their while to explore their roots again' and answers in the affirmative the question 'whether the efforts to establish a united Europe in the legal field can receive any support from our common heritage'.

[8] P. Ulmer, 'Vom deutschen zum europäischen Privatrecht?', *Juristenzeitung* 47 (1992), 1–8.

[9] R. Zimmermann, 'Der europäische Charakter des englischen Rechts. Historische Verbindungen zwischen civil law und common law', *Zeitschrift für Europäisches Privatrecht* (1993), 4–51.

law – and particularly the common law – a 'European character'. The article, which reveals a profound acquaintance with English law, should dispel any notion of it living in isolation. The author clearly believes that 'we are facing the ambitious task of elaborating a supranational, European legal unity' and intends to show that English law is not the alien and hard to assimilate 'foreign body' in the European concert it is often imagined to be. The writer concludes his contribution, which stretches from the Middle Ages to the nineteenth-century theory of contract, with expressing the 'hope that his survey of the links between civil law and common law refutes the current notion of the "isolation" of English law'.[10] Having reassured his readers about the presumed outlandish character of English law, Zimmermann proceeded in the following two years to unfold his view on the way 'European legal unity' could come about and to assign a major role to Roman law in that process. We refer to his articles 'Roman law and European legal unity'[11] and 'Civil code and civil law. The "Europeanization" of private law within the European Community and the re-emergence of a European legal science'.[12] Here the author shows how a European science of private law – preparatory to legislation – is not only conceivable, but has solid roots in past experience, both on the Continent and in England. Hence his remark that 'we should rather speak of a process of re-Europeanization' instead of 'Europeanization' and his warning that the nationalistic particularization of legal science will continue to imprint itself on the minds of the next generation of lawyers 'if nothing changes in the existing system of state examination on a strictly national basis'.

---

[10] A similar sound could recently be heard in a survey of civilian and common-law forms of process and of recent steps towards the harmonization of procedural law within the European Union: here also we find that Anglo-Scottish procedural law is not so different from continental law as 'common mythology considers them to be' (J. M. J. Chorus, 'Civilian elements in European civil procedure', *Aberdeen Quincentenary Essays* (Aberdeen, 1997), 295–305).

[11] In A. S. Hartkamp *et al.* (eds.), *Towards a European civil code* (Nijmegen, Dordrecht, Boston, London, 1994), 65–81.

[12] In the *Columbia Journal of European Law* 1 (1994/5), 63–105.

In 1995 W. Van Gerven, a professor of law with a wide experience in the European Court in Luxemburg, published his views on the possibility of a European system of 'general principles of law'.[13] The question-mark in his title displays the prudence of his approach, but does not prevent him from showing belief in the future of a European science exploring the common principles of the law. In contrast to Zimmermann, his starting points are the existing case law and treaties rather than the historic *ius commune*. The following year G. J. W. Steenhoff made a plea 'for the elaboration of a European legal science' and demonstrated that the 'weakening national differences in style of German, English and French doctrine' should not prevent this process.[14] The author reveals a remarkable acquaintance with the three aforementioned traditions and reaches some positive conclusions, without turning a blind eye to reality. He rightly refers to the work of Markesinis, a well-known bridge builder between England and the Continent,[15] and quotes Lord Bingham's expectation that England will cease to be a legal island and renew its historic contacts with 'the mainstream of European legal tradition'.[16]

In 1997 R. De Groot published an interesting editorial on a symposium held in The Hague on 28 February 1997 under the maxim 'Towards a European civil code'.[17] Already in 1994 he had drawn attention to various ways of harmonizing the

---

[13] W. Van Gerven, 'Naar een Europees gemeen recht van algemene rechtsbeginselen?', *Rechtsgeleerd Magazijn Themis* (1995), no. 10, 233–43.

[14] G. J. W. Steenhoff, 'Nationale stijlverschillen in de doctrine en de vorming van een Europese rechtswetenschap', *Weekblad voor privaatrecht, notariaat en registratie* 127 (1996), 523–9.

[15] B. S. Markesinis (ed.), *The gradual convergence. Foreign ideas, foreign influences and English law on the eve of the twenty-first century* (Oxford, 1994).

[16] 'The changing perspectives of English law', *International and Comparative Law Quarterly* (1992), 513. In a recent study, however, Lord Bingham warns against the simplistic belief that the experience and tradition of centuries can be ignored or overridden or replaced by a common code or series of codes. See Lord Bingham, 'A new common law for Europe', in B. S. Markesinis (ed.), *The coming together of the common law and the civil law* (Oxford, 2000, The Clifford Chance Millennium Lectures), 29.

[17] R. De Groot, 'European private law between Utopia and early reality', *Maastricht Journal of European and Comparative Law* 4 (1997), 159–62.

law of property in Europe.[18] Like Van Gerven he believes in a unification based on present-day case law, treaties and directives from the European Commission rather than legal science as stepping stones to the future. We can, in fact, distinguish two camps – if the word is not too melodramatic – among believers in legal unification. One puts its trust in a new *ius commune* and the strength of historic roots and antecedents, the other has less feeling for the past and hopes for a piecemeal growth of European unity through the daily work of the courts, the Commission and various political bodies: one could speak of a theoretical and a pragmatic approach.

K. Luig, in an article published in 1997, tried to build a bridge between these two schools of thought.[19] Indeed he studied the progress towards unification on the basis of the case law of the European Court of Justice, which deals with the reality of every day, but showed at the same time that in the decisions of Luxemburg a complex body of common European rules, often Roman-based and which never lost their validity, played an important role. Roman law is, in other words, not merely of historical interest, but to many jurists quite simply represents perfection. Luig consequently pleads for the use of Roman law in the preparation of a future European codification, even though certain Roman principles have had to give way to considerations based on modern natural law.

DOUBTS ABOUT A 'NEW *IUS COMMUNE*'

Let us listen now to the 'other voice' and hear what the pessimists have to say. In 1992 O. Remien voiced his strong doubts in an article with the significant title 'Illusions and reality of a European private law'.[20] While admitting that in certain fields various national systems had come closer, preparing the way to

---

[18] R. De Groot, 'Goederenrecht in de Europese Unie', *Ars Aequi* 43 (1994), 321–30.
[19] K. Luig, 'The history of Roman private law and the unification of European law', *Zeitschrift für Europäisches Privatrecht* 5 (1997), 405–27.
[20] O. Remien, 'Illusion und Realität eines europäischen Privatrechts', *Juristenzeitung* 47 (1992), 277–84.

unification, he warned that a comprehensive Europeanization is still in the distant future and has to cope with serious obstacles. He detected the beginning of a European legal science in some nuclear topics of Community law, but little else. He saw, however, real progress in contract law and civil procedure. Two years later E. Bucher frankly tackled the main obstacle, i.e. the common/civil-law dichotomy, and stressed the fundamental differences, finding the common ground marginal.[21] He underlined the difference between *Europarecht*, i.e. the positive law of the European Union, and *europäisches Recht*, i.e. European law as a whole, and warned that yielding to the temptation of minimizing the differences between English and continental law meant denying the way these two legal circles are determined by their histories, which are totally different.[22] A year later a cautionary note was sounded by Tony Weir, in an article whose subtitle – 'A skeptical reflection' – at once betrayed the author's grave doubts.[23] His starting point was the importance of language, and he found that many people nowadays underrate the obstacles the language barrier creates between European lawyers; he warned against the 'dangers of the unification of the law'. As a British jurist acquainted with the civil law – and the courageous translator of Wieacker's *Privatrechtsgeschichte der Neuzeit* into English – he obviously deserves to be listened to with great attention.

In 1996 another skeptical note was sounded across the Atlantic. In an analysis of English legal science in the seventeenth and eighteenth centuries, two American jurists analysed the English acquaintance with the writings of the civilians and

---

[21] E. Bucher, 'Recht, Geschichtlichkeit, Europa', in B. Schmidlin (ed.), *Vers un droit privé européen commun? Skizzen zum gemeineuropäischen Privatrecht* (Basel, 1994, Beiheft Zeitschrift für Schweizerisches Recht, 6), 7–31.

[22] See the discussion of Schmidlin's above-mentioned volume in *Zeitschrift der Savigny-Stiftung für Rechtsgeschichte, G.A.* 114 (1997), 460–6. In a seminar in Stockholm in 1992 R. Schulze posed the question whether legal science could lead to unification and answered that it would take a very long time before legal nationalism would be overcome (R. Schulze, 'Allgemeine Rechtsgrundsätze und Entwicklung des europäischen Privatrechts', *Juristische Theoriebildung und Rechtliche Einheit. Beiträge . . . Seminar 1992* (Lund, 1993, Rättshistoriska Studier, 19), 193–216.

[23] T. Weir, 'Die Sprachen des europäischen Rechts. Eine skeptische Betrachtung', *Zeitschrift für Europäisches Privatrecht* (1995), 368–74.

found that the use of civil-law terminology by some English writers betrayed merely superficial contacts.[24] As they put it (p. 494): 'It would seem, however, that apart from the name "Institutes" and apart from the use of the words "persons", "things" and "actions", there is very little connection between Justinian's *Institutes* and the legal writings of Hale, Blackstone, and many other English so-called Institutionalists of the seventeenth and eighteenth centuries.'

In the same year another transatlantic voice took part in the debate. This time the author was a Canadian jurist, well versed in both common and civil law, and his conclusion was an unabashed refutation of the optimistic thesis, as appeared from the very title of his article, which stated apodictically 'European legal systems are not converging'.[25] The author certainly echoed the feeling of innumerable continental lawyers when they first come in contact with English law (and vice versa): how is it possible that everything is so totally different? In a cogent demonstration which reveals his familiarity with positive law, legal history and legal philosophy the author stresses the well-nigh insuperable barriers between the law on both sides of the Channel. In his own words (p. 53): 'Given the prevalence of such a centrifugal force as nationalistic legal positivism, it is illusory to think that a common law of Europe can arise otherwise, such as through legal education or legal science', and he rejects (p. 55) the thesis that 'a new *ius commune* is in the making'. The author indicates the link between laws and cultures and *mentalités* and concludes (p. 63) that 'the common-law *mentalité* is not only different, but is actually *irreducibly* different from the civil-law *mentalité* as found in continental Europe' (whereupon he presents six specific factors).

What is the reaction of the practising lawyer to all these arguments? From numerous conversations I gathered the following impressions. That one single *Europarecht* exists is clear, as it is

[24] H. J. Berman and C. J. Reid Jr., 'The transformation of English legal science: from Hale to Blackstone', *Emory Law Journal* 45 (1996), 438–522.

[25] P. Legrand, 'European legal systems are not converging', *International and Comparative Law Quarterly* 45 (1996), 52–81.

based on the Treaties, the Directives and extensive case law. However, it deals only with disparate and specific issues, often directly linked to the economic problems of the common market. A European civil code seems unrealistic, as even on small practical points uniform regulation appears extremely difficult (see, for example, aspects of insurance law or remand in custody). The innate English aversion to codification is viewed as an insurmountable obstacle, and lawyers from the Benelux countries point out ruefully that decades of efforts to unify the law of their three countries have met with very limited success: the Kingdom of The Netherlands has recently introduced a new civil code of its own. It is admitted, on the other hand, that a European science of private law may be in the making and it is recalled that there used to be for many centuries a *ius commune* of all European jurists, using one legal language and one set of concepts, notions, categories and fundamental norms. Many continental lawyers vividly remember the cultural shock they felt when they first came into contact with the world of the common law, which, they felt, did not so much work with different concepts, as it seemed not to be conceptual at all. Even if English jurists did study Roman law, they remained loyal to their own traditions, like some famous German philologists who were world authorities on the French language, but nevertheless went on speaking German.

THE CHANCES OF LEGAL UNIFICATION

Having taken in all those views, the reader may well wonder what a legal historian makes of it all. I will try and satisfy this curiosity by presenting some reflections inspired by history (I shall afterwards try and explain what my personal position is in the pessimist-optimist controversy). The question may indeed be asked as to what the chances of a unification of European law look like in the perspective of universal history. My answer would be threefold. Firstly, history shows that in the past new large political formations have tended to evolve legal systems of their own. The whole Roman empire shared one Roman law and the whole Latin Church shared one canon law. Medieval England, which achieved and preserved political unity early on, produced a national 'common law'. France, which reached political unity much later, made big strides towards a *droit commun français* in modern times and finally achieved its aim when Napoleon published his *Code civil* in 1804. In the course of the nineteenth century Germany broke with its past of *Kleinstaaterei* and developed into a mighty Empire, which duly produced its own national civil code, made effective in the last year of that eventful century. The United States of America share the common foundation of the historic English common law; Louisiana admittedly has not joined this movement, but the common-law pressure on its civil-law roots should not be underestimated.[26]

Secondly we notice, again generally speaking, that legal science has played a preparatory, pioneering role on the road to unification. For France we need here only to mention the great names of C. Dumoulin, H.-F. d'Aguesseau, F. Bourjon and R.-J. Pothier, who wrote between the sixteenth and the eighteenth century and to whom the four authors of the *Code civil* owed so much. For Germany, the spade work done by the nineteenth-century Pandectists, who continued the tradition of the *usus modernus*, had an even profounder impact on the Code of 1900. The great issue there was the opposition between the cosmopolitan Roman and the native German tradition, a contest that was clearly won by the former (about this more in chapter 6). Is it too fanciful to compare this contest with the civil–common-law contest in the European future? And will civil law predominate there, as it did in imperial Germany, but assimilating a substantial common-law contribution (just as some traditional

---

[26] See the following recent contributions: A. A. Levasseur, 'La Réception du système de la Common Law par le système législatif français en Louisiane', in M. Doucet and J. Vanderlinden (eds.), *La Réception des systèmes juridiques: implantation et destin. Textes . . . colloque . . .* (Brussels, 1994), 381–410; S. Herman, *The Louisiana Civil Code: A European legacy for the United States* (New Orleans, 1995); S. Herman, 'The contribution of Roman Law to the jurisprudence of antebellum Louisiana', *Louisiana Law Review* 56 (1995), 257–315.

German law found its way into the *Gesetzbuch* of 1900)? Another illustration of the role of jurists in the preparation of legal unity can be found in the American Restatement of the Law. This effort by learned authors to detect and formulate the common foundation of the law of their country has already led to a certain amount of harmonization by way of legislation,[27] and European jurists have not failed to cite America as an example for their own continent.[28]

A third lesson we can learn from past experience is that science alone is not enough: the political will and political power are essential to bring the work of the scholars to fruition. In spite of the endeavours of the aforementioned jurists, France did not achieve legal unification under the monarchy. There were partial codifications in the form of major royal ordinances, but even the 'absolute kings' Louis XIV and Louis XV never achieved legal unification: they overcame neither the strength of the *coutumes* nor the ancient north–south divide. It took the personal interest and drive of a military dictator to produce the great national codes of the early nineteenth century. Similarly, it was the German lawgiver who in 1896 put an end to the bickering among the jurists and took the decisive step of the promulgation of one civil code for the whole empire.

[27] The initiative for the restatements goes back to the year 1892 when the 'National Conference of Commissioners on Uniform State Laws' was founded in order to draft codifications in the main areas of the law so that they could be taken over by the legislatures of the states. From 1923 the American Law Institute took over the task. Already in 1932 a Restatement of the Law of Contract was achieved and in 1944 the Restatement of the Law of Property, and they were followed by others. The term 'restatement' refers to the notion that the principles had already been defined by the judges, in a first 'statement'. See E. Yntema Hessel, *Unification of law in the United States* (Rome, 1947); E. Gutt, 'Le "Restatement of American Law" au xxe siècle', in J. Gilissen (ed.), *La Rédaction des coutumes dans le passé et dans le présent* (Brussels, 1962), 185–96; K. Zweigert and H. Kötz, *Einführung in die Rechtsvergleichung auf dem Gebiete des Privatrechts*, I (2nd edn, Tübingen, 1984), 292 ff.; S. Herman, 'Historique et destinée de la codification américaine', *Revue Internationale de Droit Comparé* (1995), 707–35; G. E. White, 'The American Law Institute and the triumph of modernist jurisprudence', *Law and History Review* 15 (1997), 1–47.

[28] See R. Zimmermann (ed.), *Amerikanische Rechtskultur und europäisches Privatrecht. Impressionen aus der Neuen Welt* (Tübingen, 1995). There is no need here to elaborate on the obvious importance of the United States Uniform Commercial Code.

THE PAST INSPIRES OPTIMISM

After all these presentations and generalizations the reader may well wonder what my personal feeling is and whether I count myself among the optimists or the pessimists. My somewhat paradoxical answer will be that, when I look at the present, I am a pessimist, but when I look at the past I am an optimist. Today's state of affairs is undeniably discouraging, as there are vast obstacles to legal unification among the continental countries and seemingly insurmountable differences between England and the Continent. Paraphrasing Rudyard Kipling's 1889 *Ballad of East and West* and the phrase 'East is East, West is West, and never the twain shall meet', I fear that 'civil law is civil law and common law is common law, and never the twain shall meet'. But a look at the past gives me courage, because history shows how quickly things can change and how 'wild' dreams – or nightmares – do come true. Who could have thought that the millenary unity of the Roman Church, built on St Peter's rock, would be destroyed in one or two generations and Latin Christendom be split into warring national churches and denominations? Similarly, the last country where the eighteenth century expected a disastrous revolution was France, where all observers had been struck by the popular devotion to the monarchy. In the early nineteenth century political unification in Germany seemed a pipe-dream and so did legal unification and codification. Yet by 1871 the Empire was proclaimed and in 1900 the one German civil code was introduced. In our own time hardly anyone forecast German reunification: I remember telling my students for many years that the reunion envisaged by the Constitution of the German Federal Republic was a mere *pium votum* and as unrealistic as most other pious wishes. Who foresaw that an obscure ayatollah living in exile in Paris would bring down the regime of the shah of Iran, buttressed by modern tanks and planes and immense wealth? And what about the sudden dissolution into thin air of the Soviet Union and the German Democratic Republic? The conclusion is clear: there are no insurmountable obstacles, and the most unforeseen developments do take place. In other words, if the political will is strong enough and the lawyers prepare the road, legal unification in Europe may still come about. In a minor way, certain approximations are already taking place and changes have been made in English rules and practices that were regarded until recently as immutable and based on reason. The appeal *a minima*, i.e. the appeal lodged by the prosecution in a criminal case against a lenient condemnation in order to obtain a more severe sentence in a court of appeal, used to be considered contrary to the basic principles of the common law (it still is unacceptable in the United States because of the Fifth Amendment's prohibition of double jeopardy), but this ancient and venerable rule was recently abolished and the new practice seems to be widely accepted as reasonable. Another example is the judge-made 'rule of exclusion', first established in 1769, which forbade the courts to look at what was said in Parliament to find out the intent of the lawgiver: the text of the Act and its literal interpretation according to precise and binding rules were the judges' only guides. Recently, however, with the accession of the United Kingdom to the European Economic Community (as it then was) and under the influence of the practice of the Court in Luxemburg, English judges have taken the intent of the lawgiver into account and the debates in Parliament, as recorded in Hansard, can now be quoted in court.[29]

---

[29] We refer to *Pickstone v. Freemans* (1988) and *Pepper v. Hart* (1992), *Pioneer v. Warner* (1995) and *Wagamama* (1995). The issue is still controversial. See A. E. L. Brown, 'The increasing influence of intellectual property cases on the principles of statutory interpretation', *European Intellectual Property Review* 10 (1996), 526–30. I am much obliged to Mr Anselm Kamperman Sanders for valuable information on this point.

CHAPTER 3

COMMON LAW AND CIVIL LAW: NEIGHBOURS YET STRANGERS

SIX CONTRASTING AREAS

It may be useful for a better understanding of the unification debate to proceed to a more precise and technical analysis of the differences between the common law and what the famous comparatist René David used to call the *famille romano-germanique*. We shall therefore distinguish six particular areas where the differences are both striking and fundamental, following the analysis by Peter Stein, Regius Professor Emeritus of Civil Law in the University of Cambridge and a jurist who is well acquainted with the laws of his own country and those – ancient and modern – of the Continent.[1]

But first a word of warning about the Roman law of Antiquity and the Roman or civil law of medieval and modern Europe. It is a fact that European neo-Roman law is entirely based on the Roman law as recorded in Justinian's *Corpus iuris*, but it would be a mistake to think of the classical Roman law of the great jurists, who worked centuries before Justinian put his commission of jurists to work, as looking in any way like the treatises of Bartolus and Baldus or the *Pandektenrecht* of Bernhard Windscheid (*d.* 1892). On the contrary, the Roman law of the classical period is in many respects closer in character to the English common law than to the modern civil-law systems which are derived from the medieval schools. This is because both classical Roman law

---

[1] P. Stein, 'Roman law, common and civil law', *Tulane Law Review* 66 (1992), 1591–1630. See also his *Legal institutions. The development of dispute settlement* (London, 1984), which is historical-comparative and deals with substantive law and procedure, private and criminal law, and the interpretation of statutes in England and on the Continent.

and the common law were developed through opinions and debates among experts, occasioned by particular lawsuits, rather than through general rules laid down by the legislator or theories produced by learned professors. Also in both cases legal development was centred around particular forms of action, i.e. the praetor's *formula* and the chancellor's writ. The modern civil law, in contrast, was based on university teaching and the academic study of the text of the *Corpus iuris*; it was, in other words, not case-law but book-law. The civil law is derived from post-Roman (or at least post-classical) Roman law, whereas the early common law unwittingly retraced the steps of the latter.[2]

Let us now proceed to the promised analysis of six differences between common law and civil law.

THE COMMON LAW UNCODIFIED

What could be more amazing to a continental lawyer, who can hardly imagine life without the code, than the discovery that the English common law is even at the beginning of the twenty-first century still uncodified? Before entering into this first of our six differences it may be appropriate to ponder on the exact meaning of 'code' and 'codification' (the latter term was introduced by Jeremy Bentham). Code (*codex*) is used by some legal historians in the very wide sense of a major lawbook promulgated by the lawgiver or endowed with great authority for some other reason. Thus they refer to great collections of existing norms as 'codes', a use of the term that finds some justification in Antiquity, where Justinian's collection of imperial legislation was called *codex*.[3] Other legal historians, to my mind rightly, prefer to reserve the term for the great modern lawbooks, such as the *Code civil* and

---

[2] See F. Pringsheim, 'The inner relationship between English and Roman law', *Cambridge Law Journal* 5 (1935), 347–65 (repr. in Pringsheim's *Gesammelte Abhandlungen*, I (Heidelberg, 1961), 76–50). See also F. Wieacker, 'Fritz Pringsheim zum Gedächtnis', *Zeitschrift der Savigny-Stiftung für Rechtsgeschichte* 85, R.A. (1968), 601–12.

[3] See, for example, J. H. A. Lokin and W. J. Zwalve, *Hoofdstukken uit de Europese Codificatiegeschiedenis* (Groningen, 1986).

the *Bürgerliches Gesetzbuch*, because they see a clear difference between the old 'codes', which were in reality backward-looking collections of existing texts (albeit arranged in some systematic order, revised and interpolated) and the modern code which is a forward-looking new lawbook, written as one coherent whole and intended to create a new legal order rather than to present a summary and an inventory of the old. These codes are dynamic, and collections of existing material are conservative. I therefore see an essential difference between Justinian's *Corpus* or the great canonical collections, beginning with Gratian, which are sometimes called 'codes', and the eighteenth- and nineteenth-century lawbooks that opened the modern era in Prussia, Austria, France and many other continental countries. Although England has old and venerable collections of Statutes and also some great Acts of Parliament dealing with specific legal areas (Sales Act, Married Women's Property Act) which could be called partial codifications, the English common law as such and as a whole is still uncodified. The irony of this English aloofness is that one of the most eloquent advocates of codification was the Englishman Jeremy Bentham (*d.* 1832) (whose defence of modern codes was promptly translated into French and widely read on the Continent). In spite of Bentham's appeal and the efforts of his pupil Lord Brougham (*d.* 1868), who as Lord Chancellor wielded political power, the codification of private law was not seriously attempted. Criminal law, on the other hand, got very close thanks to the efforts of Sir James Fitzjames Stephen (*d.* 1894). This great Victorian barrister with wide political and literary interests had worked on the codification of criminal law in India, where he was a Law Member from 1869 to 1872, and upon his return to Britain he undertook the codification of criminal law. His project reached the Committee stage in the House of Commons but, because of an untimely change of government in 1880, never reached the statute book. In 1877 Stephen had published a *Digest of the Criminal Law*, which could form the basis of a penal code. Consequently the Lord Chancellor instructed him in the same year to draft bills for a penal code (and a code of criminal procedure). Stephen's work was introduced into Parliament in 1878 and referred to a royal commission. But, although the Draft Code was widely praised, a change of ministry, as we said, put an end to its author's hopes (a last sign of life was given in 1882 when the procedural part was announced as a government measure in the Queen's speech).[4] The thread was picked up again after the Second World War, and a draft criminal code, prepared around 1980, was discussed by the Law Commission, a body of academics and learned barristers that advises the government, but again the text has failed so far to get on to the statute book, because Parliament cannot find the necessary time to discuss it.

In the absence of a code English lawyers have to work with old and recent statutes and case law, which explains, for example, the distinction between statutory and common-law offences, the measure of punishment for the former being based on legislation and for the latter on tradition and judicial discretion. The Bench is understandably attached to free sentencing, whereas politicians tend to favour punishment imposed by statute: the more statutory offences are created the more judicial discretion is curtailed. A few years ago, in 1996, there arose, for example, a disagreement between Michael Howard, the Home Secretary, who felt the need for a new Crime Bill (with minimum mandatory sentences – such as automatic life imprisonment for violent second offenders), and Lord Donaldson, who favoured judicial flexibility, allowing judges to take into account particular circumstances and other individual considerations (we shall return to the role of the judges later in this chapter).

PUBLIC AND PRIVATE LAW

The Continent is familiar with a sharp distinction between public and private law: lawyers are asked the routine question whether they are publicists or privatists. By contrast 'the common law is still seen as indivisible in the sense that it applies

---

[4] A. H. Manchester, *A modern legal history of England and Wales 1750–1950* (London, 1980), 44–6.

both to the government and the individual citizen, and the same courts deal with both public and private law'.[5] It is, in principle, an attractive idea that the government and its officials are under the same law and the same courts as the citizen: what could more clearly demonstrate the notion that both the governors and the governed have to live under the same rule of law? No separate administrative tribunals for the wrongdoings of the administration and ordinary courts for the citizenry, but one single network of courts for the mighty as well as the ordinary folk, manned by the same judges! In England, so the classic doctrine goes, the ordinary courts are competent for the judicial review of acts of administration: the officials of the state do not constitute a separate, privileged class. This proud concept was most eloquently expounded by A. V. Dicey (*d.* 1922), a great Victorian jurist and Oxford professor, author of an authoritative *Introduction to the study of the law of the constitution*, of 1885.[6] Although the contrast with the Continent has greatly diminished in recent years, most notably because of the growth of administrative law and special tribunals dealing, *inter alia*, with social law, it is still a real feature of the civil/common-law divide.[7] It is noteworthy that the English rejection on principle of this distinction rests on an old tradition. Sir Matthew Hale (*d.* 1676), author of the first history of the common law and himself a common lawyer of great distinction – but also well acquainted with Roman law – rejected implicitly the continental distinction between public and private law. He 'treated legal powers of "bodies politic" under the law of artificial persons' and as the king was a corporation sole, this 'had the effect of placing government within and not above, the legal order'.[8]

---

[5] Stein, 'Roman law, common and civil law', 1596.

[6] The book went through many editions. There was a tenth edition, with an introduction by E. C. S. Wade, in 1961.

[7] See now the detailed and path-breaking analysis in J. W. F. Allison, *A continental distinction in the common law. A historical and comparative perspective on English public law* (Oxford, 1996).

[8] H. J. Berman and C. J. Reid Jr., 'The transformation of English legal science: from Hale to Blackstone', *Emory Law Journal* 45 (1996), 488. See H. J. Berman, 'The origins

As soon as one opens Justinian's Institutes one is confronted with the major distinction between *ius privatum* and *ius publicum*: in ancient Rome there was a law which applied to the relations between the citizens and another law which applied to the state and its organs. The distinction was lost in the early Middle Ages, together with the Roman empire itself. It predictably resurfaced when the *Corpus iuris* was discovered and studied in Bologna and elsewhere in the West, but it made only very slow headway in the consciousness of the courts and political circles. And even when public law came of age, doctrine was for a long time – possibly until the eighteenth century – dominated by private law (which admittedly had been the field of predilection of the great jurists of the classic era, whose writings were preserved in the Digest).

It is not the case that because the distinction occurs in the lawbooks it is merely of academic interest. It went much deeper than one of those learned and subtle *distinguo*'s which the schools loved so much, because it had political overtones. The bourgeoisie wanted to mark the *ius privatum* as a safe territory for the citizen, where he had a free run, away from the structures and demands of the *ius publicum* – hence its status and popularity in the nineteenth century. But in twentieth-century communist lands, where the fate of the individual was not a priority, public law became all-important. It dwarfed private law to the point that the category had to be rediscovered in what has been called a renaissance of the *privatrechtliche Kultur*.[9] Until not so long ago private law enjoyed the greater prestige in the Law Faculties and I remember how students of my generation looked up to the great professors of *droit civil* and had little time for their unfortunate colleagues who had to teach constitutional and, even worse, administrative law, whereas criminal law had little intellectual

of historical jurisprudence: Coke, Selden, Hale', *Yale Law Journal* 103 (1994), 1651–1738. See also the relevant articles in P. Stein, *The character and influence of the Roman civil law. Historical essays* (London and Ronceverte, 1988).

9 See the article by Milan Kundera in the *New York Review of Books* of 21 Sept. 1995, who talks on p. 24 of an 'old revolutionary utopia . . . : life without secrets, where public life and private life are one and the same'.

prestige, as it was perceived as a catalogue of crimes and punishments. It is no coincidence that legal history traditionally
focused its attention on private law – I see, for example, no
criminal equivalent of Wieacker's *Privatrechtsgeschichte* or Coing's
Europäisches Privatrecht, to mention two outstanding products of
twentieth-century legal history.[10] Nor is it a coincidence that
Coing's encyclopaedic *Handbuch* is dedicated to private law, as
the very title makes clear.[11]

THE ENGLISH BENCH IS PARAMOUNT

Our third difference concerns the role and the prestige of judges.
On the Continent the courts tend to be faceless, and the judges,
instead of being highly visible individuals, have been described
as fungible persons (a reference to the *res fungibilis* in Roman law,
i.e. goods that are replaceable and interchangeable in contrast
to particular objects with a distinct value of their own).[12] By
contrast, common-law judges play a highly personal role, their
names are known to the public, they appear in the media and
their 'dissenting opinions', which may one day become the majority view, are published, discussed and often praised for their
progressive content. The aforementioned Lord Denning in the
United Kingdom and Thurgood Marshall (*d.* 1993) and William
Brennan (*d.* 1997) in the United States come to mind to illustrate this point (we will hear more of Brennan's stand on judicial

---

[10] I refer, of course, to F. Wieacker, *Privatrechtsgeschichte der Neuzeit unter besonderer
Berücksichtigung der deutschen Entwicklung* (2nd edn, Göttingen, 1967) and H. Coing,
Europäisches Privatrecht 1500 bis 1800, I: *Älteres Gemeines Recht*; II: *19. Jahrhundert.
Überblick über die Entwicklung des Privatrechts in den ehemals gemeinrechtlichen Ländern* (2 vols.,
Munich, 1985–9).

[11] H. Coing (ed.), *Handbuch der Quellen und Literatur der neueren europäischen Privatrechtsgeschichte*
(8 vols., Munich, 1973–88).

[12] The term 'fungible person' for the civil-law judge is used by Stein, 'Roman law, common and civil law', 1597, meaning 'one of a group of anonymous, almost colourless,
individuals who hide their personality behind the collegiate responsibility of the court'.
The expression *fungibele Personen* was used by Savigny for Roman jurists, at a time
when legal historians were not yet interested in their individual lives; see L. Winkel,
'Le Droit romain et la philosophie grecque. Quelques problèmes de méthode',
Legal History Review 65 (1997), 373.

review of the constitutionality of the laws and the death penalty in the following chapter).[13]

Continental jurists tend to compare the common-law approach favourably with their own, regretting, for example, that in Belgium the secrecy of the deliberation is paramount so that a judge cannot publicize his dissenting opinion, going against the view and the motivation of the majority. It is not surprising that progressive jurists plead for a modernization of court practice on the Continent, including the possibility of 'dissenting opinions' and greater openness in the motivation of judgments.[14] Continental investigating magistrates in criminal cases that captivate public opinion do, however, receive full media attention and, as was the case in Italy, may even become actors on the political scene as enemies of corruption in high places. Here is an example of a *rapprochement* in which the common law is at the giving, and the civil-law countries at the receiving, end.

THE CONTINENTAL PROFESSOR IS PARAMOUNT

In civil-law countries the 'makers of the law' have for centuries been the learned jurists led by the professors in the Law Faculties. The academic writer is the senior, the judge the junior partner in the life of the law. The authors of the great Treatises are the teachers, and all barristers and judges once sat at their feet. Legal wisdom spoke from the pages of the commentaries of Troplong, Aubry and Rau, Demolombe, Laurent and Le Page in France and Belgium, and from the *Lehrbuch des Pandektenrechts* of Windscheid in Germany. In that country the leadership of the Faculty reached its zenith with the practice known as *Aktenversendung*, in which a law court faced with a difficult question of law consulted the professors of a Law School, sent them the 'acts' of the suit and

---

[13] See M. V. Tushnet, *Making civil rights law. Thurgood Marshall and the Supreme Court 1936–1961* (New York, Oxford, 1994); J. Williams, *Thurgood Marshall: American Revolutionary* (New York, 1998); P. Irons, *Brennan vs. Rehnquist. The battle for the constitution* (New York, 1994).

[14] B. Bouckaert, *Hoe gemotiveerd is Cassatie? Pleidooi voor een waarachtig precedentenhof en een hernieuwde motiveringscultuur* (Antwerp, 1997, Thorbeckecollege, 21).

was given a binding advice. That the Bench should be told what judgement to give by a group of professors is hard to imagine in common-law lands, but on the Continent the *Aktenversendung* descended from the medieval practice of lower courts consulting a superior jurisdiction ('appeal before judgement'), as judges nowadays can pose prejudicial questions to the European courts. That, however, was consultation within the judicial system, but after the *Rezeption* German courts began to consult the law professors, whose advice eventually became binding. The most famous example was the *Spruchkollegium* of the Berlin Faculty when Savigny taught there, from 1810 onwards. The practice was terminated after 1877–9, when new laws on procedure and court organization were introduced.[15] In common-law lands the judges are the 'oracles of the law'. As to the professors, this is what Harold Laski, writing to Oliver Wendell Holmes in 1929, had to say: 'Outside one or two posts like the Vinerian professorship the law teachers are a very inferior set of people who mainly teach because they cannot make a success of the bar.'[16] One obvious reason for this state of affairs was that around the middle of the nineteenth century there was no organized teaching of English law: there were no Law Faculties. There was some teaching of Roman law through the old Regius Chairs of Civil Law, but that had no bearing on everyday life, and the old Inns of Court, where teaching had flourished in the past, had turned into cosy gentlemen's clubs. The vacuum was so glaring that something had to be done about it. But what? Several possibilities were

---

[15] See G. Buchda in *Handwörterbuch zur deutschen Rechtsgeschichte* I (Berlin, 1971), cols. 84–7; C. Schott, *Rat und Spruch der Juristischen Fakultät Freiburg im Breisgau* (Freiburg, 1965).

[16] B. Abel-Smith and R. Stevens, *Lawyers and the courts. A sociological study of the English legal system 1750–1965* (London, 1967), 183–4. Judges, according to Laski, had 'a most amusing sense of infinite superiority, and the teachers as interesting a sense of complete inferiority'. Laski might have mentioned the promising A. L. Goodhart, who was editor of the *Cambridge Law Journal* (at its foundation in 1921) and became editor of the *Law Quarterly Review* in 1926. He could, of course, not know that Goodhart would, in 1931, obtain the Chair of Jurisprudence at Oxford and turn into a leading jurist of international repute. See the Memoir on A. L. Goodhart by R. E. Megarry in the *1996 Lectures and memoirs. Proceedings of the British Academy* 94 (Oxford, 1997), 475–87.

discussed. England could, of course, organize Law Faculties in her universities and issue degrees in English law. This was the continental way, but not necessarily the best English way. Why, for example, could the old and venerable Inns of Court not be revived and invited to organize both the teaching of law and the training of practitioners? And what about the third possibility, that the profession should take in hand this teaching and training, and found something like what the *Ecole de Magistrature* was to become in twentieth-century France – with a School for Barristers and Solicitors? There is no cogent reason why lawyers had to be taught in a *studium generale* instead of some sort of technical high school for judges and barristers (as was Napoleon's ideal, who distrusted the universities and their 'ideologues'). It strikes the present-day reader as comical that the aforementioned Professor Dicey chose as the title of his inaugural lecture in Oxford 'Can English law be taught at the Universities?' (his reassuring answer was positive) – this was in 1882! Even in the twentieth century some leading lights on the Bench advised young people who had a legal career in mind to go indeed to university, but not to obtain a degree in law.[17] History, political science, philosophy, even mathematics were suitable scientific fields, but the law was no science, it was a craft which one learnt through training and practice.

Eventually the debate was settled in favour of the universities: Oxford created a School of Jurisprudence and Modern History in 1850, followed by an autonomous School of Jurisprudence in 1871. Nowadays Law Faculties are omnipresent and almost all young people who want a career as solicitor, barrister or judge obtain a law degree in a university.[18] The poverty of English jurisprudence around the middle of the nineteenth century was all the more distressing as the country could be proud of an

[17] Thus, for example, Lord Shawcross, 'Is Justice Being Done?', *Sunday Telegraph* (27 October 1963), quoted by Abel-Smith and Stevens, *Lawyers and the courts*, 369.
[18] See C. H. S. Fifoot, *Judge and jurist in the reign of Victoria* (London, 1959); P. Stein, 'Legal theory and the reform of legal education in mid-nineteenth century England', in A. Giuliani and N. Picardi (eds.) *L'educazione giuridica*, II: *Profili storici* (Perugia, 1979), 185–206.

imposing line of learned lawyers stretching from Bracton in the thirteenth to Blackstone in the eighteenth century.[19]

SUBSTANTIVE LAW AND PROCEDURE

Civil-law countries are familiar with a clear-cut distinction between substantive rules and the forms of process. There is a *Code civil* and a *Code de procédure civile*; there is a *Zivilprozessordnung* and a *Bürgerliches Gesetzbuch*. Nineteenth-century Russia even lived with a code of civil procedure (borrowed from France), but without a civil code (because tension between the Tsar and Napoleon prevented the planned transplant from French to Russian soil).

On the Continent the study of procedure as an autonomous discipline started in the twelfth century. The Romans, being good jurists, had paid a good deal of attention to the forms and formalities observed in conducting lawsuits, but they had never seen procedure as a separate branch, nor had they made it the subject of separate research and reflection: no specific book in Justinian's *Corpus* is devoted to it. Procedure became a special area of study when, in the twelfth century, jurists began to collect the procedural *membra disiecta* scattered throughout the *Corpus* and to compare them to the procedural rules in the canons and decretals of the Church. The new science, and the concomitant new practice followed by the Church courts (especially those of the modern-style bishops' officials), formed what is appropriately known as Roman-canonical procedure. The first, modest textbooks – or rather collections of excerpts from Roman and canon law – are known as the *ordines iudiciarii* and are humble efforts containing no more than a few pages. But from these slender beginnings arose a true science, which

[19] See the recent and extensive survey by Berman and Reid, 'The transformation of English legal science' and the Maccabaean Lecture in Jurisprudence by P. Stein, 'The quest for a systematic civil law', 1995 Lectures and memoirs. *Proceedings of the British Academy*, 90 (Oxford, 1996), 147–64. The author shows that some nineteenth-century treatises originated in the need to expound English law to students in India and that they sometimes led to partial codes enacted by Parliament.

already in the thirteenth century produced the vast and encyclopaedic treatise by William Durand entitled *Speculum iudiciale*, which is why the author is known to legal historians as the Speculator (which might cause some confusion in library catalogues or on the Internet). His *Speculum* was the final achievement of the creative age and remained the definitive textbook for centuries. Durand was, however, no mere academic (who studied at Bologna and taught at Modena and perhaps also at Bologna), but enjoyed an eminent career as a papal judge and administrator, and became bishop of Mende in Provence. It was during his time as papal judge that he wrote his book, which was first published in 1271 and again in 1290.[20]

In the historic common law procedure and substance were intertwined and inseparable, as the common law originated and expanded around the creation and development of royal writs. Plaintiffs could choose from a number of specific writs for specific complaints and each writ determined the progress of the case as far as summons, evidence, verdict, sentence and execution were concerned. It is significant that the first treatise on the common law, Glanvill's *Tractatus de legibus et consuetudinibus regni Angliae* (1187–9), was built around the royal writs which gave access to the royal courts and the procedures they commanded. It would be impossible to tell whether his Treatise is an exposé of substantive or procedural law. The writ of *novel disseisin* (archaic Norman French for 'recent dispossession') might illustrate how the system worked. As land and the cultivation of land were at that time as important as jobs are now, the protection of tenures against unlawful dispossession was most important, and the writ or action of *novel disseisin* was devised to implement King Henry II's policy of safeguarding the peaceful possession and cultivation of land. The writ offered a quick and efficient means of redress by the king's judges to whoever had been deprived unlawfully and without a court decision. It only applied,

---

[20] See, among recent works, L. Fowler-Magerl, *'Ordines iudiciarii' and 'libelli de ordine iudiciorum'* (Turnhout, 1993, Typologie des Sources du Moyen Age Occidental, 63).

however, within well-defined time limits (for example 'since the king's last voyage to Normandy' – in Normandy the time limit was the previous harvest but one). The plaintiff could obtain a royal order to the local sheriff to impanel a jury of twelve free and lawful men to give their verdict on the question whether he had been dispossessed 'unjustly and without judgement' by the defendant. If the verdict was positive, the defendant was fined and the land returned to the plaintiff. The action was quick and efficient because, *inter alia*, it was in the hands of a royal sheriff, no delays were accepted and the jury did its work even in the absence of the defendant. Also the mode of proof was based on a reasoned enquiry into the facts of the case and not on one of the archaic ordeals that were still widely practised at the time. The action was conducted in the margin of the traditional feudal and hundred courts, which could eventually and at leisure deal with the ultimate question as to who in the last analysis owned the land: *novel disseisin* only dealt with possession, but then 'possession is nine-tenths of the law' and the phrase *beati possidentes* is based on ancient wisdom. In course of time the scope of *novel disseisin* was widened to include the heir of the disseisor or of the disseisee or his bailiff. Other but similar writs were devised to protect a legitimate heir who was denied possession of his inheritance, and so on, until the royal writs and their respective procedures (which differed according to the moment of their creation) covered much of the law of the land. Yet, right up to the nineteenth century the English common law was still administered in the framework of the ancient writs. Although some had become obsolete and others had risen to prominence, the historic forms of action survived until a single, simplified general writ of summons in personal actions was introduced (Common Law Procedure Acts of 1852 and 1854).[21]

---

[21] See the classic analysis in F. W. Maitland, *The forms of action at common law*, ed. A. M. Chaytor and W. J. Whittaker (Cambridge, 1909). For the twelfth-century writ of *novel desseisin* see R. C. Van Caenegem, *The birth of the English common law* (2nd edn, Cambridge, 1988), 42–5.

ADVERSARIAL AND INQUISITORIAL PROCESS

The role of judge and parties is strikingly different in England and on the Continent, the former being marked by the adversarial approach and the latter by the inquisitorial. The adversarial is the early European system, whereas the inquisitorial was introduced in the wake of neo-Roman law (which, incidentally, fits in well with Lupoi's thesis I presented earlier). The adversarial procedure of the common law sees the trial as an oral contest between the parties and is controlled by them: the judge is a referee, who supervises the fairness of the proceedings in general and the cross-examination in particular, but does not himself initiate lines of questioning.[22] The parties are the active element and the judge, who is like an umpire in a match, an impartial onlooker who would not dream of actively joining the contest, the passive element. We know from legal anthropology that this is the archaic approach, especially when the struggle between the parties took on the form of a judicial combat to the death, under the watchful eyes of the judges and the encouragement of the onlookers. Under the influence of Roman-canonical procedure the role of the judge became more prominent, first in ecclesiastical courts everywhere and afterwards in the lay courts on the Continent. This was particularly noticeable in criminal cases, where the old accusatorial process, a contest between the private accuser and the suspect, gave way to the inquisitorial technique, where the machinery was set in motion by an official prosecutor and the truth of the matter actively investigated (*inquirere*) by the judge. The result was that in ecclesiastical courts one judge could at the same time and in one and the same

[22] The English judge, as Lord Wilberforce put it, acquires 'the character of a referee. He is always telling himself "I must keep out of the dispute; my only job is to see fair play, to blow the whistle when the rules are broken"', whereas the civilian judge 'thinks that it is his duty, not that of the advocate, to unveil untruths': Lord Wilberforce, 'Legal listening', *The Journal of the College of General Practitioners*, suppl. 3 to vol. 13 (no. 62), 3 at 5, quoted by J. M. J. Chorus, 'The judge's role in the conduct of civil proceedings. Some continental and Scottish ideas before 1800', *Comparative and historical essays in Scots law. A tribute to Sir Thomas Smith* (London, 1992), 32, n. 2.

case prosecute, investigate and sentence. The difference with the old common-law procedure is striking, for there the indictment was brought by the grand jury, the verdict given by the petty jury and the sentence by the judge. In civil cases the difference is not so pronounced but no less real. On the Continent, in the words of Peter Stein, 'The judge sees his function as to discover the true basis of the dispute, to bring to light all aspects of the case. All the evidence is written down and filed away. The whole proceedings, from a common-law perspective, have a rather leisurely and bureaucratic air about them.'[23] This bureaucratic character is, of course, connected with the very nature of the *ius commune* as a system of written law. Whereas continental civil procedure was less inquisitorial than its criminal counterpart, there were some notable attempts to bring civil procedure more in line with the *Instruktionsmaxime* or *Offizialmaxime* or 'principle of judicial investigation', i.e. the idea that the judge must actively intervene *ex officio* to discover the truth. The most remarkable attempt to jettison the traditional *Verhandlungsmaxime* or 'principle of party presentation', i.e. let the parties act, took place under King Frederick the Great of Prussia, who introduced the *Instruktion* (comparable to the role of the *juge d' instruction* or investigating magistrate in criminal cases) into civil proceedings, and created the *Assistenzräte*, provided by the court to take the place of the traditional barristers (who belonged to the liberal professions).[24] What Frederick had tried, however, was no more than a heightening of the active role that continental judges before him used to play in civil cases. 'There was, in J. Chorus's words, in the German *gemeiner Prozess* . . . no one-sidedly passive judge', but 'a well-balanced division of tasks between judge and parties'. The latter, he goes on, 'dominate the allegation of proof of facts and the invoking of the law on which they wish to found their claim and defence,

---

[23] 'Roman law, common and civil law', 1599.
[24] See on this short-lived experiment C. Grahn, *Die Abschaffung der Advokatur unter Friedrich dem Grossen* (Göttingen, 1994, Quellen und Forschungen zum Recht und seiner Geschichte, 2).

but the judge has a far-reaching right to co-operate both in adducing and establishing the facts and in bringing in the laws to be applied.'[25]

Although the basic difference between common-law and civil-law procedure is real enough, the reader should realize that our characterization is schematic and that reality is not as clear cut. English judges, for example, have certain powers to call witnesses, as long as there is no party objection, and they have some power to take initiatives in the conduct of proceedings without any demand by parties or counsel to do so.[26] This leads us to the concluding remark that whereas the differences between common law and civil law were and remain real enough, in several respects a *rapprochement* is undeniable.

[25] Chorus, 'Judge's role', 39.
[26] *Ibid.*, 33.

CHAPTER 4

THE HOLY BOOKS OF THE LAW

BIBLICAL AND LEGAL SCRIPTURE

The *ius commune* of the Continent was bookish law in the sense that it was based, not on native custom and accumulated case law, but on one 'legal bible', a 'holy book', the *Corpus iuris civilis*. The comparison with the real holy books of the great religions – Bible, Torah, Koran – is justified by the veneration with which the medieval glossators treated the *Corpus*, as the ultimate and authoritative revelation of legal perfection: 'reason put in writing'. We shall now analyse three examples of legal 'holy books', which were subjected to the sort of exegesis which is normally associated with the elucidation of the exact meaning of the great religious revelations. Our examples are the *Corpus iuris*, the Constitution of the United States and the *Code civil* of France.

The comparison between legal texts and scripture has been made by several scholars. The aforementioned Professor Peter Stein wrote in 1973 that the glossators regarded the Justinianic texts 'as having an almost sacred authority'[1] and in 1979 he wrote that these texts 'have been regarded from medieval times as having quasi-biblical authority'.[2] English sixteenth-century statutes were said to be 'like Scripture' and it was added that 'given the authoritative aura that surrounded the statutes, the judges would not appear to be idiosyncratic or cavalier in their exegesis' – hence the need for rules of construction.[3] The

---

[1] In P. Wiener (ed.), *Dictionary of the history of ideas*, II (New York, 1973), 691.

[2] P. Stein, *The Character and influence of the Roman civil law. Historical essays*, 3 (London, 1988, repr. of an art. first published in the *Boston University Law Review* 59 (1979), 437–51), 3.

same note was struck in connection with the great texts of the American founding fathers in a recent book by P. Maier entitled *American scripture. Making the Declaration of Independence.*[4] The same language was also applied to the French *Code civil* as 'secular scripture'.[5]

As the parallels between the Christian bible and the lawbook of Emperor Justinian are noticeable, so is the similarity between the civilians of the *Corpus iuris* and the contemporary scholastic theologians. Both were working on venerable and authoritative texts that needed elucidation and explanation in the light of their own times and needs. The comparison also applies to the sixteenth-century reaction against these medieval endeavours. Just as the Protestants rejected the medieval 'betrayal' of the original purity of Holy Writ, so the legal humanists – who used the same slogan *ad fontes* – rejected and derided the ignorance of previous Schools of Roman law and attempted to understand the laws of Justinian in their original context and their true meaning, as discovered with the help of the new historical and philological methods. In so doing they revealed the historical nature of the *Corpus iuris* as the product of a particular, past civilization and not a timeless revelation, 'fallen from heaven'. However, Protestants and legal humanists soon discovered that rejecting tradition, and restoring the exclusive authority of ancient texts, caused new problems. The pure, restored texts still needed to be studied and explained, which led to a

---

[3] C. Holmes, 'G. R. Elton as a legal historian', *Transactions of the Royal Historical Society*, sixth series, 7 (1997), 272–3: the author speaks of 'the statutes as Holy Writ: a simile very agreeable to Geoffrey Elton's views on parliamentary legislation in the sixteenth century'.

[4] New York, 1997. The reviewer in the *New York Review of Books* (14 August 1997), 37, S. Wood, speaks of profane political belief turned 'into a hallowed religious-like creed' and of secular and temporal documents being turned into 'sacred scriptures'.

[5] S. Herman, 'From philosophers to legislators, and legislators to gods: the French Civil code as secular scripture', *University of Illinois Law Review* (1984), 597–620.

multiplicity of Protestant denominations and interpretations of Holy Writ. Similarly modern lawyers and historians have understood the *Corpus iuris* in divergent ways, and many theories and schools of textual criticism have arisen (there is no need here to enter into the details of the well-known history of glossators, commentators, humanists, *usus modernus* and Pandectism).

It is obvious that 'holy books' exist in the legal as well as the religious sphere. They are, however, exceptional, as most legal systems in human experience belong to a quite different type, based on ancient custom, precedent and the accumulated wisdom of generations of *iurisperiti*. Classical Roman law is a celebrated example, and so are the common law, England's 'Old Constitution' and medieval customary law – especially feudalism – which affected the lives of countless Europeans for an entire millennium.[6] The *ius commune*, however, was different: it was a deviation from the almost universal pattern, as it was based on an authoritative book, taught and assimilated by the 'happy few' who had mastered its ancient message (in chapter 5 we will say something about the cultural climate in which this came about). The consequences for this neo-Roman law were predictable: it was strong on conceptual definitions, scholastic subtleties, refined distinctions and a theoretical and logical framework, all of which was – certainly in its initial phase – as remote from the daily life of ordinary people as it was satisfactory to scholars enamoured of a good intellectual *Spielerei*. This sort of bookish law was also, by definition, controlled by an elite of Latin-speakers, who alone understood the relevant esoteric literature.

THE AMERICAN CONSTITUTION AND ORIGINAL INTENT

It may seem a bold step to mention the US Constitution in one breath with the medieval *ius commune*, but it is not without justification. The venerable American Constitution also wields a

---

[6] See for a more detailed survey: R. C. Van Caenegem, 'Lawyers and holy books', in *Index. International survey of Roman law. Omaggio a Peter Stein*, 22 (Naples, 1994), 419–31.

quasi-religious authority and has given rise to divergent schools of interpretation and to dissensions of truly theological proportions. That ancient holy books are read with different eyes by different generations is normal, but in the case of the Constitution this divergence has direct practical consequences because of the American judicial review of the constitutionality of the laws, which makes the judicature, and particularly the United States Supreme Court, the arbiter of the law. The way this Court approaches and interprets the eighteenth-century Constitution is therefore of paramount importance; it is literally a question of life and death in the controversial issue of capital punishment, to which we will now turn our attention.[7]

The discussion in the Court concerned the fundamental question as to whether judges in the second half of the twentieth century were bound by the 'original intent' of the lawgiver of two centuries ago. One school believed that this was the case, i.e. that when a text allowed various interpretations it was the duty of the jurists and judges to discover its original meaning and the intention of the legislator, and to act accordingly. Another school held that it was unreasonable to interpret and apply a legal norm in light of the ideas and values of past centuries and that old texts should be understood and applied taking into account the 'evolving standards of decency' and the values and outlook of the present day. It is a universal issue and one encounters it, *inter alia*, in Islamic lands: when modern society is deviating from the Koran, people should be made to comply with the holy text and not the other way round. In western countries on the contrary the prevailing sentiment is that when social values change, the law should comply with the new standards and changing public opinion.

It is interesting – but not surprising – to note that this discussion is taking place also among Christian theologians. The cardinal question there is whether Holy Scripture should be studied as a historic document, with particular attention to its

---

[7] The controversy came to a head in 1967, when executions were stayed pending the decision of the Supreme Court. Executions were resumed in 1977.

meaning in biblical times, or understood as an inspiration for our own time and its message made meaningful to present generations. The most striking term used in this discussion is *Wirkungsgeschichte* ('history of effects'), i.e. a biblical exegesis that wants the ancient texts to have an effect on modern society and therefore seeks to interpret them, not in the light of their meaning two millennia ago, but of present values and aspirations.[8] A similar choice confronts learned rabbis who engage in the interpretation of Scripture. Some believe in an imaginative exegesis of the canonical texts and hold that divine words lead an existence of their own and should be applied in function of present-day conditions, whereas others pay more attention to the historical circumstances under which the Bible was written and its original intention.[9]

The issue before the US Supreme Court was the following. The Eighth Amendment of the Constitution (copied literally from the English Bill of Rights of 1689) proscribes 'cruel and unusual punishments' and as, according to the opponents of capital punishment, execution was a cruel and unusual punishment, all American laws imposing the death penalty were unconstitutional. What were the judges to decide? One school of thought maintained that it could not have been the original intent of the founding fathers to abolish the death penalty (but only unusually cruel and arbitrary means of maiming and executing), because other articles of the Constitution (the Fifth and Fourteenth Amendments), stipulating that no life could be

---

[8] See H. G. Gadamer, *Wahrheit und Methode. Grundzüge einer philosophischen Hermeneutik* (Tübingen, 4th edn, 1975; 1st edn 1960); K. Berger, *Exegese des neuen Testaments* (Heidelberg, 1977) (esp. ch. 9: 'Wirkungsgeschichtliche Hermeneutik'); P. Ricoeur, *Du texte à l'action. Essai d'herméneutique*, II (Paris, 1986); B. Vedder, 'Kennistheoretische beschouwingen bij een interpretatie van teksten in het perspectief van wirkungsgeschichtliche exegese', *Bijdragen. Tijdschrift voor Filosofie en Theologie* 49 (1988), 238–63 (Engl. summary 262–3).

[9] J. L. Kugel, for example, feels that to see scripture in the light of present-day values is more important than to fathom what its original meaning was before the rabbinical interpretations, called 'midrash', began in the first century of the present era. See J. L. Kugel, *The Bible as it was* (Cambridge, Mass., 1998) and the review by F. Kermode in the *New York Review of Books* (23 April 1998), 45–8.

taken without 'due process of law', made it clear that the law-giver had no intention of abolishing capital punishment. The opponents of the death penalty could, of course, not deny this, but they maintained that the Constitution should be interpreted in the light of standards and values of our own time, disregarding the 'original intent' if the latter was rooted in a mentality incompatible with modern society. 'Cruel and unusual punishments' are punishments that are seen as such by present-day public opinion and if it feels that executions belong to that category, they should be declared unconstitutional (whatever the feelings of the drafters of 1791). The Court, as is well known, decided against the unconstitutionality after some of the most dramatic discussions in its history (and executions, as we have seen, were resumed in 1977, after a ten-year hiatus).

We cannot enter into any details here, and we refer the reader to the eloquent article by the leading abolitionist and member of the Supreme Court, Mr Justice Brennan,[10] and to the opposing view, cogently expressed by Mr Justice Scalia, also of the Supreme Court. Scalia is known in general for his conservative stance and in particular for his advocacy of the interpretative method known as textualism, i.e. the notion that legal authority attaches to the text of a duly enacted statute or constitution. The alternative, value-oriented judicial lawmaking, leads the courts to writing their own policy preferences into the law: decision should be based on neutral principles of law rather than the values of the judges. Scalia's originalism therefore insists that the Constitution must be interpreted so as to reflect its original meaning rather than the aspirations of our own time.[11]

[10] W. J. Brennan, 'Constitutional adjudication and the death penalty: a view from the court', *Harvard Law Review* 100 (1986–87), 313–31.

[11] See A. Scalia, *A matter of interpretation: federal courts and the law*, with a commentary by A. Gutmann (ed.), G. S. Wood, L. H. Tribe, M. A. Glendon and R. Dworkin (Princeton, 1998) and the review by Robert Post in the *New York Review of Books* (11 June 1998), 57–62. The book contains the Tanner Lectures which Scalia delivered at Princeton University in 1995. It is generally known that a similar problem was discussed in twentieth-century Germany, where jurists were divided into two camps. The adherents of the 'subjective method' believed in the original intent, as it appeared

The reader might be interested to hear what my Maastricht students, who were keenly interested in this topic, thought about it in a lively discussion conducted in October 1996. They were almost unanimous in their opposition to capital punishment, but had different opinions on various points of legal detail. Some students questioned the idea that we 'should surrender to the spirit of modernity' and believed that the Constitution ought to remain unaltered and stable even, and especially when society developed new ideas and attitudes. Most, however, felt that the law had to be flexible 'as we cannot go on living in the eighteenth century'. But how was the law to be changed? Ideally, this was the task of the lawgiver (but changing the Constitution is notoriously difficult), but until this happened the judges had to adapt and interpret statutes according to modern 'standards of decency'. Whose standards of decency? Not the people's, for public opinion in the United States supports capital punishment, as does public opinion in Great Britain (at least for terrorists and killers of policemen and -women). So the 'evolving standards' are those of an elite, either the politicians who have abolished capital punishment in the parliaments of Europe, or the abolitionist judges in the United States. Some students maintained that the people were stupid and ignorant, and that it was the duty of the elite to take things in hand, a view which predictably led to heated exchanges with more democratically inclined attendants of the class.[12]

It is noteworthy that the topic of 'judicial activism' or even 'judicial supremacism' divides various countries of the

from preparatory texts and notes, whereas the followers of the 'objective method' held that ancient laws had to be interpreted in the light of modern conditions – a controversy that was taken up by Nazi jurists after 1933. See F. Rigaux, 'Les juristes allemands dans l'Etat totalitaire 1933–1945', *Académie royale de Belgique. Bulletin de la Classe des Lettres* (1995), 441–2.

[12] For more information see, *inter alia*, the following works: P. Irons, *Brennan vs. Rehnquist. The battle for the Constitution* (New York, 1994); J. Tully, *Strange multiplicity. Constitutionalism in an age of diversity* (Cambridge, 1995); M. B. Koosed (ed.), *Capital punishment*, 3 vols. (Hamden, Conn., 1996); M. Mello, *Against the death penalty. The relentless dissents of Justices Brennan and Marshall* (Boston, 1996). Even today performing artists face the comparable question whether they should respect the intent of the composer and use period instruments, as François-Joseph Fétis (*d.* 1871) believed, or follow the fashion of their own time and bring the interpretation up to date, as Felix Mendelssohn (*d.* 1847) saw it.

world-wide common-law family. American judicial review is
not popular in Britain, where Parliamentary supremacy is a
venerable tenet and 'turning judges into unelected politicians'
is frowned upon.[13] No such restraint was felt in Australia
when, in 1951, the High Court declared that the Menzies
government's legislation dissolving the Communist Party of
that country was invalid.[14] More recently the same country
caused a stir with a momentous judgment on the rights of the
aboriginals. This 'Mabo decision' of 3 June 1992 has obvious
economic repercussions, on which we will not expatiate here,
but it is remarkable from a strictly legal point of view, since it
delves deeply into historical arguments and considerations of
natural justice, with which modern lawyers are on the whole
unfamiliar.[15] The Mabo judgment, which was taken by a six to
one majority, is as significant as it is controversial. The question
was asked whether the Court carried 'judicial activism too far
in departing from principles that were thought to have been
settled for well over a century' and whether it was right to
apply contemporary standards to overturn rules formulated at
a time when community values were not necessarily the same.[16]
The 'proper limits of judicial law-making' were consequently
discussed and there was talk of Mabo as an example of 'judicial
legislation' and even 'the high point of judicial activism by the
High Court'.

[13] Thus Anthony Lester in an article entitled 'Judges and ministers' in the *London Review of Books* (18 April 1996), 9–11. The author also describes how from 'late Victorian times until the early sixties, judicial restraint bordered on judicial abdication' and quotes the argument in the House of Lords by the Home Office Minister, Baroness Blatch, that incorporation of the European Convention into British law 'would strike at the constitutional principle of Parliamentary supremacy'. This attitude has changed under Prime Minister Tony Blair.

[14] Menzies then tried to realize his aim with a referendum to amend the constitution in order to give the Commonwealth Parliament power to dissolve the Communist Party, but he lost by a very narrow margin.

[15] Text of the Mabo decision in 'Mabo and others v. the State of Queensland', *Reports of cases determined in the High Court of Australia* (1992), CLR 1, 1–217. Commentary: M. A. Stephenson and S. Ratnapala (eds.), *Mabo: a judicial revolution. The aboriginal law rights decision and its impact on Australian law* (St Lucia, Qld., 1993).

[16] The Right Honourable Sir Harry Gibbs, formerly Chief Justice of the High Court of Australia, in the Foreword to *ibid.*, xiii. The similarity with the issue in the capital-punishment debate in America is striking.

Eddie Mabo was a member of the Meriam people, the traditional owners of Murray Island and surrounding islands and reefs in the Torres Strait. In 1982 he and four other Islanders commenced an action seeking a declaration of their traditional land rights. Ten years and hundreds of pages of argument later they won their lawsuit, whose most striking elements we will briefly try to highlight. The argument went back to the eighteenth century and the European colonizers' doctrine that land in other continents inhabited by 'uncivilized' tribes was a 'barbarous country' and therefore a *res* or *terra nullius* so that the natives could legitimately be dispossessed in favour of the 'enlightened' Europeans. It is this old concept which the Australian Court, disturbing 'a legal understanding which had existed for over 150 years', rejected because, even though it had been accepted and uncontested for all those years, it offended present-day sensitivity and widespread aversion to imperialism, colonialism and racism: the dispossession which followed the annexation of the Murray Islands was 'a sordid example of discrimination which blatantly violated values embraced by the civilised world' and present-day community feelings and attitudes. Judgement according to the 'evolving standards of decency', which had been narrowly repulsed by the American Supreme Court, was a few years later accepted by a large majority of the High Court in Canberra (illustrating once again the deep divisions and uncertainties among leading lawyers of our time).[17]

THE *CODE CIVIL* AND THE SCHOOL OF EXEGESIS

The Greek word 'exegesis' meant 'explanation of authoritative but difficult texts', such as the pronouncements of the oracle. From classical Greek the term entered Christian theology, where it indicated the word-for-word explanation and elucidation of

[17] For a recent survey of this controversial issue, see M. Storme, 'Role and status of the judiciary as a state power', in *International encyclopaedia of laws. World conference* (Antwerp, 1996), 175–210.

Holy Writ: the exegete was an interpreter of God's word ('biblical exegesis'). In the seventeenth century the term was applied also to the explanation of legal texts by the philosopher Leibniz who, 'after the example of theology', distinguished four methods of learning the law, a *pars didactica, historica, exegetica* and *polemica.*[18] In the same century the term 'exegesis' appeared in English, meaning the exposition of scripture, and later more generally any gloss or explanatory note or discourse. In nineteenth-century France the term was applied to a particular method of literal explanation of the Napoleonic codes, treated as if they were as authoritative for the law as Holy Writ was for religion and as the sole source of the law. It was the legal historian Emile Glasson who called those professors, who 'taught, not the law but the Code', the 'School of Exegesis',[19] and in 1924 the civilian J. Bonnecase devoted a detailed monograph to the School, entitled *L'Ecole de l'exégèse en droit civil.* The term fitted the nineteenth-century 'somewhat superstitious' respect for the Code, which has been described as *sacralisé.*[20] It was this 'superstitious' attitude which produced a 'generation of law professors who saw themselves as having only one function, namely, the explanation of the code, article by article, following the order adopted by its drafters'.[21] Professor Aubry, in an address of 1857, maintained that it was the mission of the law professors to 'protest against any innovation tending to substitute an alien will for that of the legislator', thus betraying a truly medieval aversion to all *novitates.*[22]

Towards the end of the century the restricted and narrow approach of the School was criticized by the Scientific School,

[18] In his *Methodus nova discendae docendaeque iurisprudentiae* written in 1667, the year after he became a Doctor of Law at Altorf University, and dedicated to the Elector of Mainz (the work was printed in the following year). In the Naples edition of AD 1754 of the *Methodus nova,* in the *Thesaurus iurisprudentiae iuvenilis,* the distinction of the four parts occurs in vol. I, 21.
[19] In an address on the occasion of the one-hundredth anniversary of the *Code civil,* published in *Le Centenaire du Code civil* (Paris, 1904).
[20] See J.-L. Halpérin, *Histoire du droit privé français depuis 1804* (Paris, 1996), 45.
[21] J. M. Kelly, *A short history of western legal theory* (Oxford, 1992), 312.
[22] Quoted in Halpérin, *Histoire du droit,* 66. C. Aubry was, together with F. Rau, the author of a very influential *Cours de droit civil français* (5th edn, Paris, 1897).

which felt that other sources besides the will of the legislator were important and that lawyers should be aware of the wider social context.[23] The succession of the Exegetical by the Scientific School is in some ways comparable to what happened in the Middle Ages, when the glossators of Roman law were followed by the commentators, who dared to look beyond the confines of the very words in Justinian's lawbook and give their attention to feudal customs and urban statutes.

At first the new Civil Code was heralded as the fruit of reason itself, and a lawbook of transnational and even universal significance. These thoughts not only circulated among the French, but even German scholars believed that the Civil Code, being based on both Roman and Germanic principles, could 'claim universal validity' and lead to a 'rational development of the law on historical and national foundations'. German rejection of the Napoleonic Code as 'foreign law' was therefore unjustified, according to, for example, Heinrich Zoepfl, a professor in Heidelberg, in an article entitled 'The German element in the Code Napoléon'.[24] The discussion was not merely academic, because the Napoleonic Code was valid in German provinces to the west of the Rhine and, after French domination ended, the question arose whether this French lawbook should be retained, or replaced by German law. Defenders of the Code used its universality and its conformity with Roman and natural law as arguments against abolition.[25]

These bombastic claims should, however, not be taken too seriously as, far from being some sort of revelation from the goddess of reason, the Code of 1804 was the fruit of a protracted

[23] See the detailed monograph by B. Bouckaert, *De exegetische school. Een kritische studie van de rechtsbronnen- en interpretatieleer bij de 19de eeuwse commentatoren van de Code civil* (Antwerp, 1981) (with English summary).
[24] H. Zoepfl, 'Das germanische Element im Code Napoléon', *Zeitschrift für deutsches Recht und deutsche Rechtswissenschaft* 5 (1841), 110–32.
[25] See on all this W. Schubert, 'Das französische Recht in Deutschland zu Beginn der Restaurationszeit (1814–1820)', *Savigny Zeitschrift für Rechtsgeschichte, G.A.* 94 (1977), 182–3.

wrangle and party political in-fighting. How political Napoleon's Code was had been made crystal clear when the First Consul proceeded to a minor coup d'état to eliminate the most outspoken heirs of the Revolution from the Tribunate in order to impose 'his' code at his own dictatorial pace.

It was, however, several years earlier, under the *Directoire*, that the most passionate debate on the new civil code had been conducted, when Cambacérès's Third Project set the conservatives against the heirs of the regicides of the Convention. When one reads the speeches in the *Conseil des Cinq-Cents* and the *Conseil des Anciens*, the Parliament of the *Directoire*, one is amazed to find that 'right' and 'left' debated what was, after all, only a civil code and not a new constitution along such outspoken party lines. Although ostensibly discussing articles on divorce and the status of illegitimate children, the parliamentarians in the *Conseil des Cinq-Cents* were fighting for the new freedoms introduced by the Revolution and against the Ancien Régime and its patriarchal family.

Divorce was a great bone of contention (particularly divorce by mutual consent). To the 'left' it was a precious and lasting achievement of the Revolution and a logical outcome of the latter's ideology of liberation from various forms of lifelong constraint: they pleaded for individual freedom and attacked 'sacerdotal errors'. To the 'right' divorce by mutual consent meant the trivialization of marriage, which was the cornerstone of human society. It constituted a 'radical subversion of the social body' and incitement to 'legal prostitution'. According to one member of the *Conseil des Cinq-Cents* divorce led to *libertinage* and *débauche* and he posed the question: 'what can be more immoral than to allow a man to change his wife like changing his clothes, and a woman to change her husband like a hat?'

Even Rousseau was dragged into the debate and blamed for every evil for having described 'an imaginary state from which possibly derived all the imaginative and absurd opinions which followed the Revolution'. These politicians demanded a revision of the law in the name of the 'moral order' and protested that the Revolution had produced 'too many innovations', some of which were 'fatal to morality and society'.[26]

A few months later, in August 1797, the debate was continued in the *Conseil des Anciens*, where Portalis made a memorable speech in defence of marriage, 'a purely natural act, regulated by the civil law and blessed or sanctified by religion', 'instituted by the Creator' and 'by its destination a perpetual contract'. Divorce could, however, not be forbidden, as it was based on religious freedom, but it should only be tolerated and not encouraged by the law. Moreover Portalis attacked divorce by mutual consent on the grounds of incompatibility, because it gave 'to each spouse the baleful right to dissolve the marriage according to his or her wish'. Therefore Portalis wanted the revolutionary institutions 'which were mere forms of abuse' to be abandoned. And he even invited his fellow politicians to 'give up the dangerous ambition to make a new civil code' and to adhere to the principles of ancient Roman law 'consecrated by the suffrage of all nations'. It is ironic that this same Portalis became a few years later one of the main authors of Napoleon's *Code civil*. One also wonders if Savigny, the prophet of Roman law and enemy of codification, ever knew what Portalis had said in 1797.[27]

The debate on the status of illegitimate children was equally charged with political overtones: the first question in Cambacérès's Third Project for a civil code to be discussed in the *Conseil des Cinq-Cents* concerned the continuation of the liberal legislation of the Convention on the *droit de famille* of illegitimate children and in particular their equal inheritance rights. The latter were now said to 'favour the friends of the Revolution', which immediately politicized the discussion on the law of persons in the projected civil code. It soon became clear, however, that in 1796 the 'friends of the Revolution' were in full retreat in the *Conseil des Cinq-Cents* and that a majority was ready to

[26] Debates in the *Conseil des Cinq-Cents* in the month of Pluviôse, year V (January 1797). See J.-L. Halpérin, *L'Impossible Code civil* (Paris, 1992), 248.
[27] *Ibid.*, 252–3.

reject the liberal approach as 'subversive of all the principles of morals and the social order': even a proposal to grant illegitimate children one-third of the legitimate portion was rejected by parliamentarians who wanted to deny them any part of the parents' inheritance, in order to reinstate 'the conjugal union in its primitive purity', and the upshot of the debate was a return to the norms of the Ancien Régime, i.e. the entitlement of the illegitimate offspring to alimentation instead of a real part of the inheritance. The ensuing debate in the *Conseil des Anciens* confirmed the general political drift, with, *inter alia*, criticism of the 'chaos into which the revolutionary anarchy had thrown legislation itself': the equality between legitimate and illegitimate offspring was violently attacked by numerous orators and what has been described as a real 'crusade against criminal love, concubinage and divorce' was launched by some conservatives, whilst their opponents defended 'the sacred rights of natural children'.[28]

That the deliberations on Cambacérès's Project, presented in 1796 and containing over 1,000 articles, led only to discussion and not promulgation, should not obscure the fact that the quick results obtained by Napoleon a few years later owed a good deal to the spadework of the *Conseil des Cinq-Cents* and the *Conseil des Anciens* and their lawyer-politicians – a fact that was readily 'forgotten' after 1804. The Civil Code of that year was a symbol of national unity and was extolled as a work of genius, inspired by a man of genius, quite different from Cambacérès's Projects, which were rejected as the products of 'an incoherent and monstrous legislation'.[29] Napoleon's Code, it should be noted, was the work, not of parliament but of the government. This, together with the sincere personal interest of the First Consul, meant that its elaboration proceeded apace, unhindered by endless debates. Four lawyers were appointed to prepare a draft code in the Year VIII, the very year of Napoleon's coup d'état of Brumaire. Their work, started in August 1800, was ready by January 1801.

---

[28] See on all this *ibid.*, 240–5.
[29] Thus a propagandistic pamphlet of the Year VIII, quoted in *ibid.*, 262, n. 1.

The text was submitted to the judiciary, which made no remarks of any importance. The project was then sent to the Council of State, where it was subjected to a profound examination during a period of almost three years and 107 sessions, fifty-five of which were presided over by Napoleon. In the meantime separate sections were submitted to the Tribunate and the Legislative Corps. When it became clear that the Code had encountered some stiff political opposition, Napoleon, in January 1802, brusquely smashed this parliamentary *fronde*: he purged the assemblies of their recalcitrant elements by what amounted to a minor coup d'état (not his first), so that the submissive bodies proceeded to the vote on the thirty-six laws that constituted the Civil Code of 1804.[30]

As soon as that Code was published, all this strife was forgotten. The *paix bourgeoise* had descended upon France and a holy book had fallen from heaven. It contained the law, the whole law and nothing but the law. It symbolized peace, stability and unity. It was conservative and, as far as the law of persons was concerned, even reactionary, but it corresponded to the mood of the nation, which had turned its back on the turmoil of the recent past. It was on this firm rock that the Exegetical School was to be built.

Its protagonists were well aware that the Code suited the political climate and said so in so many words. Thus we read in J. B. V. Proudhon's *Cours de droit français* of 1810 that the Code 'is a completely new body, consisting of the wisest maxims . . . all methodically coordinated and linked in a system that suits our political situation' (*convenable à notre état politique*).[31]

It was in order to safeguard the new *état politique*, and the new bourgeois social order, that the Civil Code had to be defended against all possible forms of contamination, by Roman law,

---

[30] *Ibid.*, 273–4.
[31] Quoted by D. Grimm, 'Methode als Machtsfaktor', *Festschrift H. Coing*, I (Munich, 1982), 472, in an article devoted to the Exegetical School and its parallel, legal positivism.

canon law, ancient customs and particularly natural law. Having played its role in the subversion of the Ancien Régime, this *Vernunftrecht*, the law of reason, was now safely put away: France had had enough subversion, and natural law was only a dream which had run its course. After all, the norms of natural law are nowhere to be found in writing, so where could a judge possibly trace them?[32]

Hence the two principal tenets of the School, i.e. that the whole law is in the Code and that the literal explanation of its text is the only acceptable approach. Neither jurists nor judges should venture outside its safe parameters. As far as the learned commentaries were concerned, Napoleon – following in the footsteps of Justinian – would have preferred that there were none. This was, of course, asking too much of the learned jurists who had been writing treatises for centuries and could not suddenly give up their dearest vocation. Nor did they wait many years to go to work. The first of the four volumes of Jacques Maleville's *Analyse raisonnée de la discussion du Code civil* was published as early as 1805;[33] it was said that when Napoleon was handed a copy, he exclaimed: 'a commentary: my Code is lost'. Maleville's first volume was followed in 1808 by Delvincourt's *Institutes de droit civil français* and many others, which had in common their absolute respect for the Code, its order of articles and its terminology, and the absence of personal interpretation, philosophical reflexion or criticism, which those in power would not have tolerated. Legal history, in particular, had nothing to do with the teaching of the Faculties, nor did comparative law. Proudhon, professor and dean in the Law Faculty of Rennes, who died in 1838, expressed the feeling in terms that seem absurd in their starkness. According to him the Code was *un corps entièrement neuf* – so what was the use of ancient antecedents? – and the principles of the law should be discovered

---

[32] Thus the rhetorical question posed by François Laurent, one of the main professors of the Exegetical School, as quoted in Bouckaert, *De exegetische school*, 159.

[33] (Paris, 1805–14).

en comparant le code avec lui-même – so what was the use of comparative law?[34]

As far as the judges were concerned, some recent research has thrown new light on the subject. There is, of course, no lack of judgments which expressly proclaim the duty of the courts to apply the law. Thus, in 1836 the high court of Algiers (which had recently come under French jurisdiction) confirmed 'that it is the duty of the judges to apply existing legislation, even if there are lacunae, and that it belongs solely to the legislative power to examine and eliminate them.'[35]

Similarly, some judges stated very clearly that they applied the Code and nothing else. A judgment of 7 March 1811 by the court of Genoa, then under French jurisdiction, proclaims that 'Since, according to art. 7 of the law of 30 Ventôse of the Year XII, all ancient laws, customs, regulations and statutes have ceased having force of law in the matters encompassed by the *Code Napoléon*, it is only in the latter's letter and meaning (*esprit*) that one ought to discover the guiding principles for the decisions [of the court].'[36]

To appreciate correctly the meaning of the Code the judges naturally consulted the preparatory texts. Only the original intent was relevant and not new opinions or values entertained by the courts. Direct references to the personal will of Napoleon were sometimes used to strengthen judgments that might seem severe. Thus the imperial court of Turin strictly applied art. 214 of the Civil Code concerning the wife's duty to live in her husband's house and referred to Napoleon himself in the following terms.

---

[34] See on all this, as well as the older literature, recent reflections in R. Schulze (ed.), *Französisches Zivilrecht in Europa während des 19. Jahrhunderts* (Berlin, 1994), M. Gläser, *Lehre und Rechtsprechung im französischen Zivilrecht des 19. Jahrhunderts* (Frankfurt, 1996) and J. Gaudemet, *Les naissances du droit. Le temps, le pouvoir et la science au service du droit* (Paris, 1997), 351–3.

[35] B. Beignier, 'La conscience du juge dans l'application de la loi au début du XIXe siècle. La jurisprudence au temps de l'Exégèse', in J.-M. Carbasse and L. Depambour-Tarride (eds.), *La conscience du juge dans la tradition juridique européenne* (Paris, 1999), 279.

[36] Beignier, *ibid.*, 288.

'That is why the emperor, when during the discussion of this article in the Council of State the question arose whether the wife could even be forced to follow her husband outside the territory of the empire and in the colonies, raised the voice of his admirable wisdom against the opposite suggestion, maintaining that the obligation of the wife to follow her husband was general and absolute.'[37]

In fact, however, not all judges accepted this robot-like role. There is no lack of judgements which refer to 'natural law' or 'natural equity' (sometimes quoting the Digest as additional authority) and take the view that it was not the legislator's intent to violate the eternal rules of human or civilized behaviour. Thus a judgement of 14 February 1811 by the court of Poitiers declares that parental authority 'is a right based on nature . . . and that the civil laws have never been able to take away the rights which parents hold particularly from nature'. And the text goes on to state that 'the right to educate one's children . . . has its origin in natural law and one should, in this respect, not easily presume that the civil law wanted to deprive fathers and mothers of it, unless this was expressly stated'.[38] The reader will, incidentally, be reminded of the traditional conviction of English judges that it cannot be the intention of Parliament to enact statutes against the common law, unless it expressly says so (a very rare occurrence indeed).

Some French judges were even bold enough to refer to ancient customs and ordinances, and even to *arrêts de règlement*, abhorred by the Revolution.[39] Thus a judgement of 15 May 1824 of the royal court of Grenoble openly referred to Roman law and the older doctrine and declared 'that the Civil Code had not introduced new law' (it concerned the revocation of

---

37 *Ibid.*, 284. Napoleon had added that in case of refusal the husband could stop feeding his wife.

38 *Ibid.*, 289–90. The judgement also quoted, as an additional argument, a maxim from the Digest, *jura sanguinis nullo jure civili dirimi possunt* (rights based on blood cannot be annulled by civil law).

39 An *arrêt de règlement* was a sentence which introduced a new legal norm; it was legislation produced by the judiciary and one illustration of the power of the Parlements of the Ancien Régime.

certain alienations fraudulently agreed to by a debtor to the detriment of his creditors).[40] Similarly, on 12 July 1831, the court of Nîmes, in a case concerning the restitution of a dowry, states that 'the Civil Code has in no way innovated as far as the old rule is concerned, based on the elementary principles of the dotal system'.[41] A judgement of 27 June 1810 by the court of Nîmes invokes the 'constant doctrine within the jurisdiction of the Parlement of Toulouse'. A judgement of 1 December 1830 of the court of Grenoble maintains that when the Civil Code is silent the judges should apply 'the ancient principles', and quotes the Digest and a royal ordinance of 1735. On 17 July 1830 the same court invoked the authority of three *arrêts de règlement* of the Parlement of Grenoble of 23 August 1719, 2 April 1744 and 12 July 1754 in a case concerning a water mill.[42]

Occasionally the judges pushed their boldness one step too far and gave sentences that were blatantly *contra legem*. Thus the royal court of Lyon, on 25 February 1836, gave sentence against the law of Ventôse of the Year XI arguing that 'under the ancient legislation, a usage, confirmed by several edicts or particular regulations, authorized the drafting of notarial acts by a single notary, on condition that another notary supplied a second signature'. A few years later the Court of Cassation felt obliged to annul this sentence, however reasonable, and whatever ancient legislation and usage had said about it.[43]

---

[40] Beignier, 'La conscience du juge', 284.

[41] *Ibid.*, 288. As is well known, the discussions about the northern 'community of goods' (joint estate of husband and wife) and the southern dotal system were heated. The *Code civil* introduced the community, known as the *régime légal*, but left the southerners the liberty to choose the Roman system if they wished. See on this J. Brisset, *L'adoption de la communauté comme régime légal dans le Code civil* (Paris, 1967).

[42] Beignier, 'La conscience du juge', 287.

[43] *Ibid.*, 288. On 19 January 1831 the court of Bordeaux, in a criminal case, referred to the attitude 'of all civilized nations' regarding the respect for the ashes of the deceased (*ibid.*, 290).

CHAPTER 5

WHY DID THE *IUS COMMUNE* CONQUER EUROPE?

THE RE-ROMANIZATION OF THE WEST

That western Europe would one day discover Justinian's law-book was to be expected: renewed contact with the Greek world and the Crusades – *inter alia* to Constantinople – would have seen to that. And one can suppose that the discovery would have stirred interest and caused academic discussion, comparable to present-day studies of the law of the Egyptian papyri or the Assyrian clay tablets. It was, however, far from self-evident that the 'rebirth' of the *Corpus iuris* in the twelfth-century School of Bologna would be the start of a triumphal march that would change the legal face of Europe. Why should the discovery of the laws of a bygone civilization affect the West so deeply? And why should the previously unknown lawbook of a Byzantine emperor, who had ruled over a tiny part of the Latin world, change the character of Western law? This hi-jack of medieval European law by Justinian's *Corpus iuris* is both so amazing and so important that its causes deserve to be analysed in some depth.[1] It is obvious that this romanization – or re-romanization – of western law, which covered eight centuries and numerous countries, was not caused by one single factor: complex influences were at work, which we shall now proceed to analyse.

---

[1] I decided to delve into this problem because of questions asked in 1995 by my Maastricht students, who remarked that the existing literature carefully described what happened, but seldom addressed the question of the causes.

LEGAL CAUSES

There was, to begin with, a purely legal cause, i.e. the intrinsic quality of the *Corpus iuris* and the medieval teaching it produced. European law in the eleventh and twelfth centuries was archaic, feudal, provincial, harking back to the Germanic tribal past, and administered orally. Very little was put in writing, and of law schools, lawbooks and legal treatises there was very little: only some poor, unsophisticated and shapeless attempts, guided neither by central legislation nor by great central law courts. The *ius commune*, by contrast, offered everything the archaic 'first feudal age' lacked. Its great lawbook contained the best the Romans, the most gifted jurists the world had ever seen, had written down. Its language was elegant and technical, the norms and ideas clearly formulated and presented in a structured, systematic way: the sheer quality of the Digest was bound to dazzle people who were looking for the best law available. The teaching of the Schools produced professional jurists, Roman-canonical procedure demanded professional judges, and papal legislation, often emanating from law professors, sustained the rise of a law, as required by logic and progress. To people who were used to parochialism, the universality of Roman law must have been impressive: here were a legal system and a legal science that had belonged and could belong again to the whole civilized world. The vision arose of a law that was timeless and literally utopian, in the sense of belonging to no particular place. The definition of contract and of the obligations it creates, and the enumeration of the other sources of obligations – these were abstract and self-evident data, which seemed to flow from reason itself and to be equally valid in ancient Beirut or medieval Bologna and Orleans. What a shock people must have felt who compared the helpless and shapeless attempts of the *Leges Henrici Primi* to present, in 'Latin' that was understandable for Anglo-Normans, the Old English dooms with the Institutes of Justinian or the writings of such classical jurists as Modestinus or Ulpian![2] And how revealing was the

---

[2] The *Leges Henrici Primi* are an English lawbook of *c.* 1116–18, edited by L. J. Downer (Oxford, 1972). Another English lawbook of the same time and probably by the

discovery of a court procedure based on rational enquiry and ignorant of the ordeals of water and iron and judicial combat (which was not much more than a slightly camouflaged fight to the death between the parties in 'litigation')!

POLITICAL CAUSES

Quality by itself is not enough to make legal innovation acceptable to society at large: the political will of those in power is also most important. It so happened that in the twelfth and thirteenth centuries the 'common learned laws' of the Faculties provided intellectual ammunition to the ecclesiastical and secular leaders who were building modern, centralized power structures. Popes, kings and regional princes were leaving the archaic feudal age behind and erecting the well-ordained and forcefully led organizations that became typical of modern Europe. It is obvious that the message of the late imperial *Corpus iuris* fitted their plans perfectly, as it was full of the majesty of the state and the unlimited power of the emperor, who 'was not bound by the laws' and whose 'pleasure had the force of law'. These axioms, applied to the medieval kings (who were 'emperors in their own kingdoms'), were a welcome support for their endeavours at unification and centralization. The technical training in the Schools moreover provided Church and state with professional lawyers who could run the daily administration of the reinvigorated monarchies. 'Here emerged', in Berman's words,

'for the first time strong central authorities, both ecclesiastical and secular, whose control reached down, through delegated officials, from the center to the localities. Partly in connection with that, there emerged a class of professional jurists, including professional judges and practising

same author is the *Quadripartitus*. See on the complex problems posed by both works: P. Wormald, 'Quadripartitus', in G. Garnett and J. Hudson (eds.), *Law and government in medieval England and Normandy. Essays in honour of Sir James Holt* (Cambridge, 1994), 111–47. Wormald, p. 113, comments on the relative neglect of the collection and thinks that 'the barely penetrable opacity of [the author's] Latin' may be one reason for it.

lawyers. Intellectually, western Europe experienced at the same time the creation of its first law schools, the writing of its first legal treatises, the conscious ordering of the huge mass of inherited legal materials, and the development of the concept of law as an autonomous, integrated, developing body of legal principles and procedures. The combination of these two factors, the political and the intellectual, helped to produce modern western legal systems, of which the first was the new system of canon law.'[3]

The *Corpus iuris* favoured a centralized and hierarchical state and an organized, streamlined bureaucracy. It was a monument to the 'descending theory of power' and provided a model for what the papacy and the monarchies were trying to achieve.

Illustrations of this interplay are not difficult to find. During the first years of his reign the German King–Roman Emperor Frederick I Barbarossa had subjugated the rebellious city of Milan and the rest of his north Italian kingdom. In so doing he was supported not only by the swords of his knights, but also by the new legal science. At the meeting at Roncaglia in 1158 the Bolognese professors had proclaimed, with Justinianean texts in hand, the fullness of power of the emperor, the *dominus mundi* who knew no equal. 'It was', in Ullmann's words, 'at the Diet of Roncaglia that the ideological alliance between the Staufen empire and the Roman lawyers of Bologna was cemented'.[4] This same emperor issued a decree in favour of the law students of Bologna, the famous authentic constitution *Habita*, which granted laymen who studied Roman law the same privileges as were enjoyed by the clerics who studied canon law. The imperial government, 'which held itself to be a successor of the ancient caesars', understood the need for 'an

---

[3] H. J. Berman, *Law and revolution. The formation of the western legal tradition* (Cambridge, Mass., 1983), 86.

[4] W. Ullmann, *A short history of the papacy in the Middle Ages* (London, 1972), 191. It is amazing to see how an Italian legal historian visualized this event. Writing of Frederick's hatred of the communal movement, Calasso described him as 'this German emperor who at the Diet of Roncaglia in 1158 had the illusion he could revert to the *status quo ante* in the name of a legality which consecrated his despotism of a crowned barbarian and ignored real life' (F. Calasso, *Medio evo del diritto*, 1: *Le fonti* (Milan, 1954), 413).

adequate supply of properly trained personnel, and this training could evidently be had only at the advanced level provided
by Bologna'.[5] In the next century Frederick II, the last great
Hohenstaufen emperor, founded in 1224 the university of
Naples, which was specifically expected to provide imperially
minded lawyers and to train the ruling class of his kingdom
of Sicily. In the following year diverse measures in favour of
his new university were taken by the emperor who 'aspired to
nothing less than creating a great intellectual elite to sustain the
imperial throne with the instruments of law and the prestige of
culture'.[6]

Towards the end of the thirteenth century the powerful king
of France, Philip IV the Fair, was employing his legists, i.e.
lawyers who had studied the *leges* of the Romans, in order to
support his quest for full sovereignty throughout his kingdom.
Like their predecessors at Roncaglia they used the *leges*. This time
it was against the aged count of Flanders, Guy de Dampierre,
who was involved in a bitter conflict with his royal suzerain
and who, to 'imperial' eyes, represented the old feudal order
and was oblivious to the unique majesty of the state and the
potestas regia: it was significant that the count was condemned
by the Parlement of Paris for *laesio majestatis*, a typically Roman,
anti-imperial offence.[7] Around the middle of the thirteenth century the French jurist Jean de Blanot, whom we mentioned in
chapter 1, had shown how feudal principles could be eliminated
by appealing to Justinian's lawbook. He vigorously denied that
a vassal had to help his lord against the monarch because this
'insurrection against the king' would be an offence under the old

---

5 W. Ullmann, *Law and politics in the Middle Ages. An introduction to the sources of medieval political ideas* (London, 1975), 93. Barbarossa decided to incorporate *Habita* in Justinian's
  Code, emphasizing that he was the successor of the Roman emperors of Antiquity.
6 P. Nardi, 'Relations with authority', in H. De Ridder-Symoens, *A history of the university
  in Europe*, I: *Universities in the middle ages* (Cambridge, 1992), 88.
7 J. R. Strayer, *The reign of Philip the Fair* (Princeton, 1980), 324–46. On politics and legal
  science see the recent survey by L. Mayali, 'Lex animata. Rationalisation du pouvoir
  politique et science juridique (XIIe–XIVe siècles)', in A. Gouron and A. Rigaudière
  (eds.), *Renaissance du pouvoir législatif et genèse de l'Etat* (Montpellier, 1988), 155–64

Roman *lex Julia maiestatis* (Dig. 48, 4; Cod. 9, 8), which protected the *magistratus populi romani*.[8]

The renewed papacy under Gregory VII and his successors was also close to the teaching of Bologna. The science of canon law, which was founded there, was indebted to the civilians, as no canonist was worth his salt without thorough grounding in the *Corpus iuris civilis*. The imperial hierarchy of ancient Rome was a source of inspiration for its late medieval counterpart in the papal *curia*. And when the ecclesiastical courts were modernized, around AD 1200, their judges, the episcopal officials, were invariably university graduates. Modern government and neo-Roman law lived in symbiosis, in the Church as much as in the kingdoms.

If the *ius commune* influenced the modernization of government, it did not cause it: things had started to move before the *legum professores* were teaching and their pupils manning the councils of state and the law courts. The point is worth making, because the highly visible impact of the Schools might easily create the wrong impression. The 'great leap forward' started with the Gregorian reform, which aimed at wringing the *libertas ecclesiae* from the kings and princes. In so doing it established the undisputed supremacy of the pope over the whole Latin Church. The success of the movement and the consequent separation of Church and state caused such a profound change that H. J. Berman, in his aforementioned *Law and revolution*, argued that the traditional names of the 'Gregorian reform' or the 'investiture struggle' are inadequate and that 'papal revolution' is better suited to indicate the real impact of this 'first major turning point in European history'. This 'papal revolution' was prepared and launched by Pope Gregory VII, first as a member of the *curia* (AD 1050–73) and then as pope (1073–85). These events were

---

[8] The 'king of France being emperor in his kingdom, because he recognizes no superior in temporal matters', this imperial law applied to the Capetian rulers. See M. Boulet-Sautel, 'Jean de Blanot et la conception du pouvoir royal au temps de Louis IX', in *Septième centenaire de la mort de Saint Louis. Actes des colloques de Royaumont et de Paris (21–27 mai 1970)* (Paris, 1976), 57–68, esp. 67.

well ahead of the School of Bologna and its 'Four Doctors'. Not long afterwards several states similarly entered the road to modernization through the strengthening of the central government, the organization of local administration and the rationalization of judicial procedures: the 'Anglo-Norman empire', the county of Flanders and the Norman kingdom of Sicily were the pioneers on the road to modern statehood, soon followed by Capetian France. All this was going on in the twelfth century at a time when the Schools were just beginning to find their way and with little or no help from their graduates: neither King Henry II of England (1154–89) nor Count Philip of Flanders (1157–91) were surrounded by legists. Things changed, as we have seen, in the thirteenth century, but what had come first was the political will to modernize government; once that programme was launched, it gratefully used the intellectual support of the schoolmen and their treatises. Modern statehood was produced not by Justinian, but by rulers who wanted to provide orderly government and by their subjects who wanted efficient administration. The intellectuals and the sophistication to carry the reforms through came, however, to be largely provided by the *ius commune* and the two Faculties of Roman and canon law.[9]

CULTURAL CAUSES

It is time to turn our attention to the cultural context. C. H. Haskins called the pivotal age 'the Renaissance of the twelfth century' and even people who reject the proliferation of 'renascences' will admit that this was indeed a great intellectual century. Western Europe discovered numerous Greek and Arabic works of science, which were being translated into Latin, analysed, explained and confronted with traditional beliefs. So great was the admiration for the newly discovered revelations from Antiquity that they were treated as absolute authorities. As the Bible contained the truth in matters of religion, so

9 The reader will find a recent collection of related studies in T. N. Bisson (ed.), *Cultures of power. Lordship, status, and process in twelfth-century Europe* (Philadelphia, 1995).

did Aristotle, Galen and Ptolemy in logic, physics, anatomy, astronomy and geography. Truth was discovered, not through observation but through correct understanding of the Ancients, the 'giants' upon whose shoulders the medieval 'dwarves' were sitting. It was no different with jurisprudence. Here also one great authority from Antiquity contained the ultimate perfection in legal science, so the best way to become a jurist was to assimilate the timeless revelation of the *Corpus iuris*. In this climate of obedience to ancient authority the Christian Middle Ages had to overcome the objection that it was of pagan origin. In the case of Aristotle these qualms were overcome by ascribing to him an *anima naturaliter christiana* and as far as the great Roman jurists of the classical era were concerned, who were all pagans, all doubts were overcome by the consideration that their writings were part and parcel of the lawbook promulgated by a great Christian emperor. So the way the *Corpus* became the object of veneration and literal explanation fitted perfectly into the general approach of the age to the giants from Antiquity (and, of course, to the holy books of Christendom).[10]

ECONOMIC CAUSES

Around the twelfth century Europe entered a new phase in its economic development, marked by greater productivity, urbanization, the rise of a market and money economy, industrial and commercial expansion, increased circulation of goods, persons and services, sophisticated banking and a lively international trade. Italy took the lead and the rest of Europe followed: in the later Middle Ages the early-medieval model looked more and more archaic and – sooner in southern and western, more slowly in central and eastern Europe – receded into the past. The feudal world of priests, manorial lords and rural serfs had gone or was on the way out. The new urban money economy

---

[10] See two useful surveys in M. Clagett, G. Post and R. Reynolds (eds.), *Twelfth-century Europe and the foundation of modern society* (Madison, 1961); R. Benson and G. Constable (eds.), *Renaissance and renewal in the twelfth century* (Cambridge, Mass., 1982).

created a favourable environment for the study of Roman law. Urbanization allowed the concentration of large communities of doctors and students in universities, which were invariably located in cities and towns, whereas higher productivity and monetary expansion freed a larger proportion of the population from labour on the land. Moreover, the expansion of trade and industry led to a heightened interest in the workings of contract (sale, barter, credit, delivery of goods, correct pricing and so on), whereas the urban population looked for more peaceful and efficient forms of dispute settlement than the judicial combat favoured by the knights in earlier days. The *Corpus iuris* was the product of a highly developed cosmopolitan economy and was clearly more suited to the emerging West of the later Middle Ages than the customs of the closed agricultural and manorial world of the motte-and-bailey castle.

That a developed economy was favourable for the emerging Law Faculties does not mean, however, that it needed them. Urbanization had not waited for the Schools to take off and the success of the new international market-economy would have been real even without the rediscovered *Corpus iuris*. Irnerius and the Four Doctors did not gloss the lawbook because the Italian merchants asked them to. All over Europe the expansion of commerce took place without Justinian and the merchants developed their own mercantile customs, which were applied in their own commercial courts, notably in the great international fairs of Champagne. It is no coincidence that when French commercial customary law was eventually codified under Louis XIV, the Ordinance on Commerce of 1673 was mainly the work, not of a learned lawyer but of a merchant, Jacques Savary.[11] For centuries, therefore, commercial life and the teaching of the Schools went their own separate ways and the Latin-speaking clerics who agonized over divisible and indivisible obligations lived in another world than the clients of the Piepowder courts. It was only after the School of the Commentators had turned

---

[11] Louis XIV's *Ordonnance sur le commerce* is also known as the Code Savary. See for a recent survey J. Hilaire, *Introduction historique au droit commercial* (Paris, 1986).

its attention to the practical needs of its own time that the *ius commune* became directly relevant and eventually affected the contracts and obligations current in every-day life.

OPPORTUNISTIC CAUSES

We are referring here to the fact that soon after the surfacing of the Digest in northern Italy advocates and judges began quoting from it in order to win their cases or to justify their judgements. This had nothing to do with theory or legal science or the urge to master the contents of a great lawbook: the only concern was to find arguments in difficult lawsuits. If his case did not go well, a clever lawyer could always try and impress local judges by quoting from an ancient lawbook ('ancient law was good law'), issued by a great Christian emperor. This universal ploy of desperate pleaders was resorted to very soon after the *Corpus* had found its way to northern Italy and must have encouraged both advocates and judges to take a closer look at this new star in the legal firmament.

We shall now present some north Italian cases from the last quarter of the eleventh and the first half of the twelfth century, where rules or terms from the *Corpus iuris*, which betrayed some degree of acquaintance with its norms and terminology, were quoted. We naturally open the series with the famous judgement of Marturi (near Poggibonsi) of AD 1076, conserved in a contemporary *brevis recordationis*, a rather informal written record. We shall strictly limit ourselves to the features that are relevant here, and not enter into the numerous intricacies of what Bruno Paradisi has called 'una pagina tormentatissima della storia giuridica'. In March 1076 in a court of Beatrix, countess of Tuscany, a lawsuit was conducted concerning some land and a church in a place called Papaiano between the advocate and the provost of the monastery of St Michael in Marturi, plaintiffs, and one Sigizo of Florence, defendant. The plaintiffs claimed the land on the ground of an ancient donation, but the defendant said that he was entitled to it by a forty years' prescription.

The plaintiffs replied that during that time they had tried in vain to gain access to a magistrate in order to suspend the running of the prescription, whereupon the judge gave sentence in their favour and ordered, as a temporary measure, the *restitutio in integrum* (full restitution). He did this on the basis of a passage in the *Digestum vetus* (the oldest part of the Digest known in the West), to which a lawyer, referred to as a *legis doctor,* had drawn his attention and which said that the praetor promised *restitutio in integrum* to people who had not been able to gain access to a magistrate.[12] Consequently the defendant, in a separate document, gave up his claim. The case is rightly famous as it was the first time for centuries that the Digest was quoted in an Italian lawsuit. The Digest had been copied in southern Italy and soon afterwards became known in the north. Although this case and the following are still quite exceptional, they highlight the appearance of the *Corpus iuris* in the law courts some time before Irnerius and the other Doctors started their research and teaching.[13]

Our next example comes from Garfagnolo where, in AD 1098, in another lawsuit opposing local laymen to a monastery, in this case St Prospero in Reggio Emilia, the advocate of the church quoted from Justinian's Code (7, 37, 1–3) and Institutes (2, 6, 14). A few years later, in a lawsuit in Rome, in AD 1107, between one Cintius, dispenser of the monastery of Saints Cosmas and Damian, and one Peter, concerning the rent of some land,

---

[12] The judgement of 1076 reads as follows: 'lege Digestorum libris inserta considerata per quam copiam magistratus non habentibus restitutionem in integrum pretor pollicetur'. The corresponding text is Dig. IV, 6, 26, 4 which quotes the Twelfth Book of Ulpian's *Ad Edictum* and says: '. . . et si magistratus copia non fuit, Labeo ait restitutionem faciendam' (if no magistrate had been available [to suspend the running of prescription] Labeo said that restitution should nevertheless be ordered).

[13] The two most recent studies of the Marturi case (where the reader will find references to the copious older literature) are: B. Paradisi, 'Il giudizio di Marturi. Alle origini del pensiero giuridico bolognese', *Atti della Accademia Nazionale dei Lincei, Classe di scienze morali, storiche e filologiche. Rend. Mor. Acc. Lincei,* series IX, vol. V (Rome, 1994), 3–21 and F. Theisen, 'Die Wiederentdeckung des römischen Rechts im Alltag des 11. Jahrhunderts dargestellt an einer Urkunde von 1076', *The Legal History Review* 62 (1994), 127–43.

reference was made to the Institutes (4, 6, pr.), the Digest (4, 3, 7, 8 and 44, 7, 51) and the Code (7, 39, 3).[14]

In the first half of the twelfth century several legal terms from the *Corpus iuris* which had previously been unknown made their appearance in the city registers of Milan, as was the case in other regions of Italy.[15]

THE *IUS COMMUNE* A GOOD THING?

During the discussion of the causes of late medieval enthusiasm for Justinian some students wondered whether it had been a gain or a drawback for European law. Many legal historians would treat this as a naive question, as it is not deemed to be the scholar's task to pronounce value judgements. The discussion, moreover, would have to start with the baffling question of what is good or bad law, which is felt to be more appropriate for a class on legal philosophy. It seemed nevertheless that it would be interesting to dive into a bit of 'counterfactual history' and to wonder what would have happened if the School of Bologna had not existed. What would Europe and European law have looked like if the *Corpus iuris* had been confined to the lecture rooms and the seminars of obscure savants and never ventured outside their halls and libraries? Some readers will be inclined to dismiss this as vain speculation: how can we possibly know what would have happened if something which did happen had not happened? The point is that the impact of Roman law did take place, and for the non-speculative mind this should be enough. However, I believe that in this case our answer would not necessarily be purely speculative, because we have the English common law to give us a realistic indication – based on observable fact and not on mere imagination – of what would normally have happened

---

[14] A. Padoa Schioppa, 'Il ruolo della cultura giuridica in alcuni atti giudiziari italiani dei secoli XI e XII', *Nuova Rivista Storica* 64 (1980), 273–8.

[15] A. Padoa Schioppa, 'Aspetti della giustizia milanese dal X al XII secolo', *Atti dell'11° congresso internazionale di studi sull' alto medioevo, Milano 26–30 Ottobre 1987*, I (Spoleto, 1989), 542.

if the whole of Europe had, like England, produced a modern, adequate legal system without the help of the School of Bologna. Until the twelfth century the whole of Europe shared the same archaic feudal customs, but then society began to move towards a more adequate and rational law. On the Continent this was eventually achieved through the assimilation, in varying degrees, of the 'learned written laws', whilst in England it was done through the creation, by royal judges, of an advanced national system, using native materials[16] such as the royal writs and the jury.[17] I believe it is not an unreasonable contention that without Bologna the Continent also might well have taken this same road. There too the central courts of the emerging nation states would have developed modern judge-made systems of law, using native institutions. There too legal theory would have been a marginal and late afterthought in a practice-oriented world. The law of contract, for example, would not have started with the theoretical exposés of Roman and scholastic thinkers, but would have ended with a doctrine of contract after centuries of practice. Such, as is well known, was the fate of contract in England, where, in the words of Grant Gilmore, 'the common law had done very nicely for several centuries without anyone realizing that there was such a thing as the law of contracts . . . The idea that there was such a thing as a general law – or theory – of contract seems never to have occurred to the legal mind until Langdell somehow stumbled across it.'[18] Alternatively the great royal courts might have worked on the basis of one particular customary law: the court of the Châtelet produced a modern law for the Paris area and the Parlement might slowly have imposed this *coutume de Paris* as the norm for a unified French law. Whatever way the Continent took, its law would have looked – for better or worse – very different from what exists today. There

---

[16] I here follow the thesis of M. Lupoi, *Alle radici del mondo giuridico europeo. Saggio storico-comparativo* (Rome, 1994).
[17] See R. C. Van Caenegem, *The birth of the English common law* (2nd edn, Cambridge, 1988).
[18] G. Gilmore, *The death of contract* (Columbus, Ohio, 1974), 3. The reference is to C. C. Langdell's *Casebook on Contract* of 1871.

would have been more national systems, as Europe would have lacked the cosmopolitan learning of the Schools, and those laws would have been based on custom and the case law of superior courts rather than legal theory.

GRAECA NON LEGUNTUR

While we are on the speculative path, it might be the right moment to say something about the absence of the Greek law of Antiquity in the make-up of the medieval *ius commune*. The question here is why something did not happen that might very well have happened. The query is by no means fatuous, since it was in the line of logical expectation that Greek law would have intrigued the West. After all, Greek law was interesting for its own sake, being democratic and speculative and the product of the famous Athenian city-state. It also belonged to a civilization that fascinated medieval scholars, who could never have enough of Plato, Aristotle and other Greek scientists, mathematicians, geographers and anatomists. So the question why Greek law left the western Middle Ages indifferent is a reasonable one to ask. Not much has been written about it, because historians are naturally inclined to write about what happened rather than what did not. This is a pity, since the absence of certain events, ideas, reactions or feelings can be revealing, if only we give it our attention.[19]

Several reasons come easily to mind why the medieval jurists ignored Greek law. The most obvious is that the Latin West in general 'did not read Greek' (*graeca non leguntur*). The School of Bologna ignored even the original Greek text of certain recent imperial constitutions in Justinian's lawbook, which were replaced by the old Latin translations from the *Authentica*.[20]

[19] The reader will find some considerations on that topic in H. E. Troje, 'Europa und griechisches Recht' (Frankfurt, 1971, inaug. lect.), and H. E. Troje, Graeca leguntur. *Die Aneignung des byzantinischen Rechts und die Entstehung eines humanistischen Corpus iuris civilis in der Jurisprudenz des XVI. Jahrhunderts* (Vienna, Cologne, 1971).

[20] F. Wieacker, *Privatrechtsgeschichte der Neuzeit* (2nd edn, Göttingen, 1967), 134; P. Koschaker, *Europa und das römische Recht* (Munich, Berlin, 1947), 106.

Hattenhauer, however, believes that 'it is all too easy to explain
the aversion of medieval jurists to Greek legal texts by their
linguistic ignorance'. He points out that in the north Italian
cities, which had numerous links with Byzantium, Greek was
indispensable, as 'it was a language of great importance in commerce, politics and law'. The author goes on to explain that
Greece and Rome were not only estranged but had become
enemies; 'in the West Greek thought had turned into heresy',
wherefore 'the phrase *graeca non leguntur* . . . was the expression of
a strict self-imposed tie with the spirit of Rome and the Digest'.[21]
There is doubtless a good deal of truth in this, but why did this
aversion to all things Greek not stop the Latin West studying
Greek philosophy and Greek science – in translation – with true
passion? When thinking people were interested in Greek and
Arabic science, they procured the necessary translations and
went to work, teaching, commenting (and sometimes being accused of heresy). What stopped the jurists obtaining translations
of the laws of Hellas and the reflections on law and justice in the
Athenian democracy? Roman law admittedly had the enormous
advantage of being available in one comprehensive and systematic collection; there was nothing like it for Greek Antiquity. But
when one sees with what zeal medieval intellectuals looked for
sources of information and ordered and digested them, one can
hardly doubt that, had they wanted to, they could have come up
with some interesting witnesses of ancient Greek law in order
to comment and lecture on them.[22] One cannot help feeling
that something more visceral was to blame, i.e. a fundamental
political preference for Imperial Rome over democratic Athens.
Neither the feudal barons, nor the emerging papal and royal

---

[21] H. Hattenhauer, *Europäische Rechtsgeschichte* (2nd edn, Heidelberg, 1994), 259.
[22] Anyone who needs convincing of the richness of Greek law and its monuments should
consult the two following bibliographies in J. Gilissen's *Introduction bibliographique à
l'histoire du droit et à l'ethnologie juridique*, A/7: *Grèce (à l'exclusion de la période hellénistique)*
by G. Sautel, and A/8: *Monde hellénistique* by J. Modrzejewski (Brussels, 1963, 1965),
693 and 544 titles. The reader will find a handsome survey in ch. 2 and 3. 'La Grèce
classique' and 'L'Epoque hellénistique', in J. Gaudemet, *Institutions de l'Antiquité* (Paris,
1967), 145–250.

monarchies could find any justification or inspiration in Athens, but the monarchies found plenty of useful material in Justinian's lawbook and they were happy to employ lawyers trained in the *leges.* On the other hand the Romans had produced more gifted jurists, particularly in the field of private law, than the Greeks, who surpassed them in philosophy and the arts but could not rival them in the subtle definition of legal rules and principles: for the teachers of private law in the medieval Schools Greece had nothing to offer comparable to the Digest.

So strong was the appeal of Greek philosophy that when, in the last two centuries of the Middle Ages, urban democracy and anti-papalism became vigorous, the intellectuals, such as Marsiglio of Padua (*d.* 1343) turned, not to Greek law, but to Aristotle for inspiration.

CHAPTER 6

LAW IS POLITICS

THE 'REALIST SCHOOL'

That law and legal science are part of the cultural landscape is obvious. The 'makers of the law' do not operate in a void. They belong to a particular society and are influenced by the intellectual climate and the great debates of their time. It is therefore natural that in the preceding chapters we have talked of the impact of ideas and 'holy books' on European legal history. This cultural aspect is, however, only one part of the story, as power politics and economic pressures also mark the face of the law: legal history is *Machtsgeschichte* as well as *Ideengeschichte*, and the *Struggle for law*, to quote the title of a famous book by Rudolph von Jhering,[1] is far from being an academic issue to be debated in some learned colloquium. It has rightly been said that 'law is politics under another guise' and the 'critical legal studies movement' or 'Realist School', which was influential in the 1970s and 1980s, deserves credit for drawing attention to this other side of the coin of legal history. The representatives of this American realism, in Kelly's words, 'denied to law and judicial decisions any special character separating them from politics and political decisions'. Without going so far as to hold that law was no more than a device for maintaining structures favourable to the ruling class, they held 'nevertheless that law is politics under another guise, and its pretensions to objectivity, transcending political commitments, are a sham'.[2]

---

[1] An English translation of Jhering's *Der Kampf ums Recht* was published with an Introduction by Albert Kocourek in Chicago in 1915 and reprinted in the *Legal Classics Library* in New York in 1991.

[2] J. M. Kelly, *A short history of western legal theory* (Oxford, 1992), 432.

It is our intention in this last chapter to pursue this aspect of legal history in depth, using as a sort of case study the elaboration and promulgation at the end of the nineteenth century of the German Civil Code, an enduring internationally recognized monument of European science and legislation.[3]

GERMAN UNIFICATION AND THE CIVIL CODE OF 1900

In the early nineteenth century Germany found itself in a dramatic predicament. Having emerged victorious from the 'wars of liberation' against Napoleon, it faced several political and legal options. Should the country, which still consisted of numerous kingdoms, principalities and free cities, be united into one German nation state? If so, should this new Germany be an autocratic monarchy or a liberal republic? Should it be *grossdeutsch* or *kleindeutsch*, in other words should it contain all people of German language and culture, including the Austrians, or should the Habsburg monarchy, with its Slav, Magyar and Latin ethnic groups, be excluded as not really belonging to the German nation? These were burning questions and we are reminded of the present predicament of the European Union, where the similar problem as to how extensive it ought to become and which countries in the East can be considered European is posed. The next issue was, of course, whether the projected German nation state should have one national civil code, which seemed to be logical and to follow Bavarian, Prussian and Austrian precedents as well as the famous French model. And if there was to be a civil code for the whole of Germany, was it to be based on Roman law, as represented by the *usus modernus pandectarum* (consequent to the *Rezeption*), or should it turn its back on this foreign import and embrace native traditions and be truly German? The question of political unification was settled by the proclamation

---

[3] This *Bürgerliches Gesetzbuch*, promulgated in 1896 and effective as from 1900, was admired in France by R. Saleilles and F. Gény (a French translation appeared in 1904) and in England by F. W. Maitland, and taken as a model for the civil codes of Japan, Switzerland and Turkey.

in 1871 of the German Empire, without Austria. And, after the acrimonious debate between Savigny and Thibaut, the advocates of a national civil code won the day in 1896, as we have seen. We shall briefly recall the dispute on codification as such, and then discuss more at length the question as to what sort of a code was eventually desirable for Germany.

C. F. von Savigny, a conservative German patriot of French Huguenot descent and one of the founders of the Historical School, abhorred codification and believed in the naturally evolved and ever-developing law of the people, as expounded by aristocratic and learned jurists, the natural leaders of the nation. Codification, the fixing of norms at one particular moment, could only thwart the natural course of the law, which was sure to live in osmosis with changing needs and values. His main opponent, A. F. Thibaut, by remarkable coincidence also of French Huguenot descent, believed in codification on principle. He belonged to the rationalist, Enlightenment tradition and was a liberal cosmopolitan. He defended legislation imposed by far-sighted rulers and their elitist councillors. He wanted the law to be written down in the vernacular and made accessible to the common man, not a secret science for the initiated who read Latin. Savigny, who reacted violently to Thibaut's plea for a national code, found the idea 'scandalous' and loved pointing out the technical imperfections of the *Code civil*, whereas he held legal science based on Roman law to be vastly superior.[4]

There were some strange contradictions in Savigny's attitude: how could the law, rooted in the *Volksgeist* and in the romantic idea of the German nation, be based on Roman law, a notorious transplant? And how could professors who believed in the cosmopolitan *ius commune* be best placed to interpret and develop the historic law of the people? The fact is that the famous

---

[4] Thibaut's 1814 appeal was entitled 'Über die Nothwendigkeit eines allgemeinen bürgerlichen Gesetzbuches für Deutschland', and Savigny's reply, published in the same year, was entitled 'Vom Beruf unsrer Zeit für Gesetzgebung und Rechtswissenschaft'.

Professorenstreit was not only, or even primarily, about technical merits or academic considerations, but was fuelled by deeply felt political convictions and patriotic gut reactions. Savigny distrusted laws and codes decreed by revolutionary assemblies or upstart military dictators (especially when they were French) and he much preferred the accumulated wisdom of generations of jurists, as interpreted by aristocratic law professors, as he was himself. Thibaut did not adore plebeian assemblies either, but he liked the notion of a code embodying the ideals of the eighteenth-century natural law, the universalist appeal of the Enlightenment and the certainty provided by comprehensive codes. The clash between the two jurists was about politics rather than academic merits or legal technicalities.

GERMANISTS AND ROMANISTS

Thibaut's appeal eventually won the day and the young German empire quickly undertook the task of providing the new nation state with national codes, of which the Civil Code was to be the crowning achievement. Yet, if the decision in favour of the Civil Code was quickly taken, the debate on its contents and roots was prolonged and lively. Two camps, as we have seen, vied with each other – the defenders of native tradition and those of Roman law; they were known as the *Germanisten* and the *Romanisten*. Both groups studied the past, but they held separate congresses and published separate periodicals, or at least separate sections of one periodical, i.e. the *Germanistische* and the *Romanistische Abteilung* of the *Savigny Zeitschrift für Rechtsgeschichte* (both wings operated in the name of Savigny, who indeed was both a Romanist and one of the founders of the German Historical School of Law).[5] The Germanists studied the Germanic *Volksrechte* and medieval German customs, borough charters and

---

[5] Vol. I of both the *Germanistische Abteilung* and the *Romanistische Abteilung* of the *Zeitschrift der Savigny-Stiftung für Rechtsgeschichte* appeared in 1880. They succeeded the *Zeitschrift für geschichtliche Rechtswissenschaft* (1815–50) and the *Zeitschrift für Rechtsgeschichte* (1861–78).

lawbooks in order to discover the roots of true German law. The Romanists studied the *Corpus iuris* and the Schools to which it had given rise in medieval and modern Europe and especially in post-*Rezeption* Germany, in order to build a system of private law that was technically perfect and the best basis for the law of a German empire that was destined for great achievements. Neither group was moved by purely antiquarian or speculative curiosity or interest in the past as such, as they both saw their respective fields of study as contributing to the quest for the best Civil Code for their country: the legal past was directly relevant to the legal future. Both camps conducted their research with earnestness and erudition: it is hard to realize nowadays what enormous efforts went into the critical edition of Roman-law texts – first and foremost the ultimate edition of the *Corpus iuris civilis* itself – and of medieval charters, capitularies and law-books – many of which are still used in every legal history seminar today. Since both the Roman and the German tradition could boast impressive monuments, both camps had solid arguments for their convictions. And whereas medieval texts appear to us often clumsy and awkward in comparison with the subtlety and elegance of the Roman law of Antiquity and the fluency and technical precision of its Latin, who would be bold enough to proclaim apodictically the ultimate superiority of either of the two elements that nourished the *droit romano-germanique* which so deeply marked our world?

The famous nineteenth-century debate on German and Roman law nowadays belongs to the past – as does the debate about codification (at least on the Continent). However, some rumblings can still be occasionally overheard at legal history conferences, where, on the whole, both customary and the 'learned written laws' are unemotionally studied as any other historical phenomenon. I still remember my surprise when, at a conference in Paris many years ago, the late Professor Pierre Timbal, who led a team at the Archives Nationales in Paris to study the registers of the Parlement of Paris, in a sudden outburst criticized his fellow legal historians for paying too much

attention to the *ius commune* and the medieval Law Faculties and
neglecting the study of customary law, which, as he rightly observed, 'was the law that regulated the daily lives of the vast
majority of our ancestors, who had never heard of Bartolus or
Baldus'. And is it too far-fetched to compare the German debate
on the Germanic and Roman ingredients of their future code to
the present debate (which we presented earlier) on the possible
integration of civil-law and common-law elements in a future
European private law?

NATIONAL FEELINGS

No matter how strongly scholars disagreed about the merits of
native vs. Roman law, their contest would not have been so dramatic if other, unacademic, i.e. political, considerations had not
been involved. The quarrel was so violent because it concerned
political feelings. It was all about the very touchy issue of national against foreign law: what could have been more burning
in the young, proud nation state? National pride, the ethnic interpretation of history and the romantic *Volksgeist* theory formed
a potent current from the late eighteenth century onwards. It
was opposed to the rational cosmopolitanism of the Enlightenment. Möser, Herder and Hegel come to mind in Germany, and
in France Montesquieu believed that the French aristocracy, to
which he belonged, descended from superior Frankish warriors,
whereas the peasants proceeded from the vanquished inhabi-
tants of Roman Gaul. And although the *gemeines Recht* had been
predominant in Germany for a long time, the old native tradition
was far from extinct, particularly in Saxony, an ancient princi-
pality which became a kingdom in Napoleonic times: Saxon law
was partially accepted as a subsidiary norm (*gemeines Sachsenrecht*)
right up to the *Bürgerliches Gesetzbuch*.[6] So both camps could
legitimately appeal to the past.

---

[6] Nor should we forget that right up to 1900 the French *Code civil* had been followed in
the German territories west of the Rhine. See R. Schulze (ed.), *Französisches Zivilrecht
in Europa während des 19. Jahrhunderts* (Berlin, 1994).

THE 'SOCIAL QUESTION'

Roman law was not only attacked for political, patriotic reasons, it was also accused of being unsocial. Socialism was gaining ground in Bismarck's Germany – much to the Iron Chancellor's alarm – and social concerns were lively also in various parties of Christian inspiration. It was therefore natural that the German vs. Roman controversy was also conducted in the light of the debate on community feeling vs. individualism. German law was seen by its defenders as socially conscious, ethical, warm and community-oriented, as appeared from the very title of the work of one of its main advocates, Otto von Gierke's *Das Deutsche Genossenschaftsrecht.*[7] Gierke was one of the great German jurists of the nineteenth century and the spokesman *par excellence* of the Germanist camp. He was, as we shall see later, a critic of the Civil Code that was being prepared, an antagonist of legal positivism and a defender of the ethical foundations of the law and of its social role: in 1889 he gave a lecture on 'the social mission of private law' ('Die soziale Aufgabe des Privatrechts'). After some years in Breslau and Heidelberg, he had an illustrious career in the Berlin Law Faculty during one of its most glorious periods and was therefore involved in all the great issues of legal science and legal politics – notably the social question – of Wilhelmine Germany. Gierke was also interested in the German contribution to the rise of modern natural law, as appeared from his work on Althusius of 1880.[8] The main object of his criticism was, as could be expected, Roman law. Not, however, that of Antiquity, but the *usus modernus* and the *Pandektenrecht* of his own

---

[7] The term is difficult to translate. *Genossenschaft* means 'community' or 'society' and *Genossen* are 'comrades', so the general idea is of free corporations of comrades or good neighbours. The (unfinished) work appeared in four volumes between 1868 and 1913. The *Genossenschaftsrecht* sees German law as the bond that held families, rural and urban associations, the Church and finally the German state together in a free 'give and take' and was inspired by a strong community feeling.

[8] *Johannes Althusius und die Entwicklung der naturrechtlichen Staatstheorien.* Althusius, or Althaus (1557–1638), was a German lawyer and political theorist and a convinced Calvinist and democrat. He defended popular sovereignty against state absolutism, developed a theory of the social contract and was an advocate of political pluralism based on divinely inspired natural law.

time, in which he detected an 'atomizing and individualistic'
approach, which was a threat to the 'popular German and social private law' that the German empire needed. No wonder
therefore that economic liberalism was another object of his
aversion. Indeed, in contrast to the good old law of the German
past, Roman jurisprudence was seen by the Germanists as cold,
egotistical, materialistic and close to capitalism and *laissez faire*
economics. It was therefore understandable that the exaggerated individualism, i.e. the absence of social concern, of the first
draft of the Civil Code was blamed on Roman law. That this
draft did not get into the statute book was, *inter alia*, because of
Gierke's onslaught in his *Der Entwurf eines bürgerlichen Gesetzbuchs
und das deutsche Recht* (1888) and in his aforementioned 'Die soziale
Aufgabe des Privatrechts'(1889). Gierke's criticism had little effect on the final text of the *Bürgerliches Gesetzbuch*, but was influential in the long run in different political and social circumstances,
when 'the social drop of oil' was increasingly appreciated.

Belief in the opposition between the 'individualistic Roman'
and the 'social Germanic' spirit and the notion that the *Rezeption*
was 'a national misfortune' only gained credence in the second half of the nineteenth century, as earlier generations of
Romanists and Germanists had been united by their faith in
political and economic liberalism. The Germanists of that time
saw no opposition between their love of old German liberty and
the prestige of Roman law. That in the sixteenth century some
German authors were opposed to the *Rezeption* was based on the
different fear that the administration of justice was falling into
the hands of foreigners or Germans who had been brainwashed
in Italian and French universities – a well-known xenophobic
theme.[9] The 'social drop of oil' is still a bone of contention today. The reader will remember the row about the Social Chapter

---

[9] See on all this the detailed analysis by K. Luig, 'Römische und germanische
Rechtsanschauung, individualistische und soziale Ordnung', in J. Rückert and
D. Willoweit (eds.), *Die Deutsche Rechtsgeschichte in der NS-Zeit. Ihre Vorgeschichte und
Nachwirkungen* (Tübingen, 1995), 95–137. See also J. Rückert, 'Die Rechtswerte der
germanischen Rechtsgeschichte im Wandel der Forschung', *Savigny Zeitschrift für
Rechtsgeschichte*, G. A. 111 (1994), 275–309.

in the Treaty of Maastricht, to which the British Government objected so strongly that an opt-out clause was provided to allow Britain to adhere to the Treaty after all. In the 1930s the social concerns of Roosevelt's New Deal were equally controversial. And the reader will, of course, be reminded of a similar debate in imperial Russia. Here some authors lauded the ancient communitarian spirit of village life in the *mir* (and the protection and solidarity it gave the peasants and their families) in contrast to the selfish poison of western individualism, whereas liberal, western-minded intellectuals naturally berated the *mir* for its stifling traditionalism and peasant backwardness.[10]

THE 'FORESTS OF GERMANY'

It is noteworthy that in the field of constitutional law the nineteenth century witnessed a comparable debate – in Germany, England and the United States – on the merits of the ancient Germans as the founders of modern political freedoms. Numerous authors traced parliamentary liberalism back to the celebrated *forêts de Germanie* (to use the famous expression in Montesquieu's *Esprit des lois*, book XI, chapter. 6): the freedoms of modern constitutions originated with the Germanic nations of the early Middle Ages, especially the Anglo-Saxons. By contrast, Roman law, absolutism and centralization were depicted as the arch-enemies, nor could the Roman Church and its papal centralism count on any sympathy from Protestant legal historians. The German idea that 'in such forests liberty was nurtured' found a favourable response in nineteenth-century England, particularly in the last third, when it was advocated by such famous medievalists as W. Stubbs, J. R. Green and E. A. Freeman. Already in 1870 Stubbs had found the roots of the English constitution 'in Germany', a thesis he elaborated in the first volume of his *Constitutional history of England* (1874). England, he found, was the purest example of Germanic attitudes, characterized by

---

[10] See some recent reflections on this old theme in S. Schmemann, *Echoes of a native land: two centuries of a Russian village* (New York, 1998).

freedom and self-government, which had been weakened but
not extinguished by Norman rule. In the romantic *Short history
of the English people* of 1874 Green situated the origins of the
English constitution in Lower Germany, between the Elbe, the
Ems and the Rhine, and he too found in Anglo-Saxon England
the purest Teutonic organization, untainted by Roman influence. Freeman, in his *History of the Norman conquest of England*, of
1867, waxed positively lyrical in the description of the effects
of primeval Germanic democracy (which he thought he had
seen in action during a visit to Switzerland). This successor of
Stubbs in the University of Oxford saw the Germanic compo-
nent as predominant, not only in the Anglo-Saxon period but
throughout English history. He was particularly fond of the 'self-
governing Teutonic community' in the ancient *Marken*. There
was a real Anglo-German alliance in the struggle against the
idea of the leading impact of Roman law on Europe. American
historians took the theme a logical step forward. Since their
free institutions had English roots, their Constitution was also
bound to reflect the Teutonic past. This was indeed the idea defended by the American historian Herbert Baxter Adams, who
had studied in Germany, in a lecture to the Harvard Historical
Society on 'The Germanic origin of New England towns', in
1881,[11] whose conclusions seemed natural to many listeners and
probably reflected the *communis opinio* at the time. They were in
any case echoed by such leading jurists as Melville M. Bigelow,
James Barr Ames and Oliver Wendell Holmes.[12]

THE CIVIL CODE BECOMES LAW

Germanist criticism eventually proved of no avail against the
promulgation of the German Civil Code, not even, as we have

[11] Published in the *Johns Hopkins University Studies in Historical and Political Science*, vol. II
(1882).
[12] See on all this the detailed analysis by M. Reimann, '"In such forests liberty was
nurtured". Von den germanischen Wurzeln der anglo-amerikanischen Freiheit', in
G. Köbler and H. Nehlsen (eds.), *Wirkungen europäischer Rechtskultur. Festschrift für Karl
Kroeschell* (Munich, 1997), 933–51.

seen, the protest by Otto von Gierke. The process of codification had begun in 1874, barely three years after the proclamation of the second Reich. By 1888 a first draft was ready in the Reichstag, but it was criticized for being too professorial. It was indeed heavily indebted to Roman law in the guise of the Pandectists, led by Bernhard Windscheid, who taught at Leipzig from 1874 to his death in 1892 and was a prominent member of the first Commission for the Civil Code from 1874 to 1883 (some critics called its project the 'little Windscheid'). However, when the Code was finally passed by the German Parliament in 1896, it appeared not to differ substantially from the initial draft. Generally speaking the Code was most strongly supported by learned jurists, the top officials in the Department of Justice and the industrialists, who liked its bias towards the freedom of contract. Its technical qualities were undeniable but, unlike the *Code civil*, it was a learned code for learned judges and lawyers and not meant to be bought in pocket-sized editions by masses of enthusiastic citizens (as had been the case in France in 1804). The only consistent opposition in the Reichstag had come from the social democrats. Their attitude had been not obstructionist but constructive, as they had proposed ninety-four amendments, mostly based on Gierke's ideas. They failed, however, to get any of their main objectives on to the statute book.[13] The German Civil Code, effective in the last year of the nineteenth century, was the result of opposing political convictions and scientific arguments.[14]

[13] See on this point D. Brandt, *Die politischen Parteien und die Vorlage des Bürgerlichen Gesetzbuches im Reichstag* (Heidelberg, 1975); T. Vormbaum, *Sozialdemokratie und Zivilrechtskodifikation* (Berlin, New York, 1977); G. Bender, 'Die Ablehnung des BGB durch die sozialdemokratische Reichstagsfraktion', *Rechtshistorisches Journal* 3 (1984), 252–67; H. Hofmeister (ed.), *Kodifikation als Mittel der Politik. Vorträge und Diskussionsbeiträge über die deutsche, schweizerische und österreichische Kodifikationsbewegung um 1900* (Graz, Cologne, 1986); H. Schulte-Nölke, *Das Reichsjustizamt und die Entstehung des Bürgerlichen Gesetzbuchs* (Frankfurt, 1995); T. Repgen, 'Die Kritik Zitelmanns an der Rechtsgeschäftslehre des ersten Entwurfs eines bürgerlichen Gesetzbuchs', *Savigny Zeitschrift für Rechtsgeschichte, G. A.* 114 (1997), 73–127.
[14] See, for the period up to the 1860s: J. Q. Whitman, *The legacy of Roman law in the German romantic era. Historical vision and legal change* (Princeton, 1990), and for the following

CIVIL CODE OR THE PEOPLE'S LAWBOOK?

Criticism of the new Code did not disappear with the passing of the century, but continued in the next, not only in academic circles, but also in the party political arena. Here the Code and its Roman orientation became the object of virulent rejection at the hands of the National Socialist Party, which undertook – but never achieved – the elaboration of a new code, to be known as the *Volksgesetzbuch*, or 'people's lawbook'.

As early as 1920 the tone was set in art. 19 of the programme of the National Socialist German Workers' Party, which said: 'We demand the replacement of the Roman law, which serves the materialistic world order, by a German community law.'[15] When, thirteen years later, the NSDAP, or Nazi Party, came to power, it lost no time in trying to implement this legal aspect of its ideology, and work was taken in hand to replace the Roman-inspired *Bürgerliches Gesetzbuch*, which could mean a 'bourgeois' code as well as a 'civil' code, by a 'people's code' or 'people's lawbook'. The drafting of this *Volksgesetzbuch* was entrusted to the Academy for German Law, founded on 26 June 1933 and manned by academic jurists.[16] It worked under the guidance of Dr Hans Frank, who afterwards became notorious as the ruler of German-occupied Poland.[17] The new code never saw the light of day, but the reports and projects drafted by the Academy

decades: M. John, *Politics and the law in late nineteenth-century Germany. The origin of the Civil Code* (Oxford, 1989).

[15] See the detailed analysis in P. Landau, 'Römisches Recht und deutsches Gemeinrecht. Zur rechtspolitischen Zielsetzung im nationalsozialistischen Parteiprogramm', in M. Stolleis and D. Simon (eds.), *Rechtsgeschichte im Nationalsozialismus* (Tübingen, 1989), 11–24. The German text reads as follows: 'Wir fordern Ersatz für das der materialistischen Weltordnung dienende römische Recht durch ein deutsches Gemeinrecht.' It should be noted that *Gemeinrecht* has nothing to do with the historic *gemeines Recht*, or *ius commune*, but can best be rendered as 'community law'.

[16] H.-R. Pichinot, *Die Akademie für Deutsches Recht. Aufbau und Entwicklung einer öffentlich-rechtlichen Körperschaft des Dritten Reiches* (Kiel, 1981); D. L. Anderson, 'The Academy for German Law 1933–1944', 2 vols. (Michigan, 1982, Diss.).

[17] C. Schudnagies, *Hans Frank. Aufstieg und Fall des NS-Juristen und Generalgouverneurs* (Frankfurt, Bern, 1989); D. Willoweit, 'Deutsche Rechtsgeschichte und "nationalsozialistische Weltanschauung": das Beispiel Hans Frank', in Stolleis and Simon (eds.), *Rechtsgeschichte im Nationalsozialismus*, 25–42.

have survived and are being edited so that they can be studied.[18] Public opinion was left in no doubt about the importance of this legal revolution. The German Lawyers' Conference, or *Deutscher Juristentag*, in Leipzig in 1933, which attracted some 20,000 participants, had chosen as its theme 'German law and its struggle against foreign law' – the latter being, of course, Roman law. In this conflict between 'lawyers' law' and 'people's law' the idea of fundamental rights of the individual was rejected and the general good was given precedence over individual interests. The impact of Hitler's becoming Chancellor on 30 January 1933 was quickly visible, as the membership of the League of National Socialist Lawyers rose from 1,374 on 1 January 1933 to almost 30,000 in October of that year. The congress at Leipzig witnessed the proclamation of Hans Frank as *Reichsrechtsführer*. There was a march with torches, an address by Frank devoted to the impact of 'Nordic man' in China and Persia, and a speech by Hitler himself.[19] This, however, did not mean that the Führer had given up his old mistrust of lawyers. As his regime became ever more dictatorial, respect for legal norms came to reach an all-time low so that, in the summer of 1942, even Frank became worried and gave lectures in the universities of Berlin, Vienna, Munich and Heidelberg protesting against the arbitrary exercise of power: he rejected the fashionable criticism of lawyers and exclaimed that 'without the law society was impossible'. He was promptly dismissed from his post as President of the Academy, which was put under the authority of its old competitor, the

---

[18] Volume I of the *Volksgesetzbuch*, containing the General Principles and Book I (devoted to the law of persons), in the form of a 'project and explanation', was presented in Munich and Berlin in 1942 by J. W. Hedemann, professor at Berlin, H. Lehmann, professor at Cologne and W. Siebert, professor at Berlin, as no. 22 in the series *Arbeitsberichte der Akademie für Deutsches Recht*. The edition by present-day scholars of the materials of the Academy for German Law has been undertaken by W. Schubert, W. Schmid and J. Regge, who published vol. 1 of the series *Akademie für Deutsches Recht 1933–1945. Protokolle der Ausschüsse* in Berlin and New York in 1986. In 1941 J. W. Hedemann had published a short report under the title *Das Volksgesetzbuch der Deutschen. Ein Bericht.*

[19] P. Landau, 'Die deutschen Juristen und der nationalsozialistische Deutsche Juristentag in Leipzig 1933', *Zeitschrift für neuere Rechtsgeschichte* 16 (1994), 373–90.

Ministry of Justice. The latter's head, Otto Thierack, henceforth was both Minister of Justice and President of the Academy and lost no time in warning the academicians that 'the creation of the law was no science and no purpose in itself, but a task of political leadership and ordering'; the efforts of the Academy 'had to be based at all times on the political aim outlined by the political leadership'.[20] It is evident that not only private, but also public law, as well as legal history were deeply affected by the new regime in Germany.[21]

The plebeian Nazis were not alone in their onslaught on Roman law. Respectable academics also voiced criticism in the twentieth century, as they had done in the nineteenth. In their ranks we find cultural historians such as the famous Oswald Spengler, who criticized the Civil Code of 1900 and deplored the rediscovery of the *Corpus iuris*, and leading legal historians such as Heinrich Mitteis. This internationally known specialist in feudalism and the comparative study of medieval political institutions was also an authority on the history of German private law. He did not sympathize with the Nazis, who cold-shouldered him and thwarted his professorial career,[22] but he was a German patriot, who had studied under Gierke in Berlin and believed in the values of the Germanic past as a source of inspiration for twentieth-century Germany: legal history had to illustrate the great deeds of the German nation and to make youth proud of its exalted past. Mitteis consequently was critical of the *Corpus iuris* and the *Rezeption*, even though his father, Professor Ludwig Mitteis, was a renowned student of Roman law. Heinrich Mitteis reproached the *ius commune* with 'partly

---

[20] See on all this H. Hattenhauer, 'Das NS-Volksgesetzbuch', in A. Buschmann *et al.* (eds.), *Festschrift für Rudolf Gmür* (Bern, 1983), 255–79.

[21] See on all this the thoughtful work of M. Stolleis, *Recht im Unrecht. Studien zur Rechtsgeschichte des Nationalsozialismus* (Frankfurt, 1994)

[22] Mitteis started teaching in Cologne in 1920, moved to Heidelberg in 1924, and in 1934 to Munich, where he ran into trouble with Nazi students. So he moved to Vienna in 1935, only to meet trouble again in 1938: he was suspended and threatened with protective custody. He was finally dispatched to the obscurity of Rostock university. After the war he taught in Berlin, Munich and Zürich.

destroying' the flourishing German community law:[23] because of the *Rezeption* 'modern German law was no more a possession of the people, but an esoteric science in the hands of bureaucrats'. Roman law 'had put an end to the social sense of the historic German law and dealt a blow to a flourishing German community law'.[24] Mitteis's career and ideas are a striking illustration of the interaction between law and politics.[25] That politics were the driving force behind the *Volksgesetzbuch* is evident enough, but it is striking that even the Nazis could not obtain what they wanted without the aid of the learned jurists: the Academy for German Law looked like a professors' club.

The present-day observer is amazed that Roman law was blamed for the triumph of capitalism and anti-social *laissez faire*, for the demonstration of the falsehood of this idea was easy to make. One had only to consider the case of nineteenth-century England, where freedom of contract and *laissez-faire* liberalism triumphed as nowhere else, and it all happened under the aegis of that most un-Roman of legal systems, the English common law![26] But how could such a 'cold', 'Roman' counterproof prevail against deep-seated political convictions?

JURISTS IN THE THIRD REICH

As several students wanted to know more about the impact of Nazi rule on German lawyers, I decided to devote some extra time to answering their questions. This I did by presenting five jurists – four of them legal historians – who, to varying degrees, sympathized with the new regime, i.e. Fehr, Feine, von Schwerin,

---

[23] *Deutsches Privatrecht* (3rd edn, Munich, 1950), 46.
[24] K. Luig, 'Begriff und Aufgabe des Deutschen Privatrechts in der Sicht von Heinrich Mitteis', in P. Landau, H. Nehlsen and D. Willoweit (eds.), *Heinrich Mitteis nach hundert Jahren (1889–1989)* (Munich, 1991), 97–9.
[25] See G. Brun, *Leben und Werk des Rechtshistorikers Heinrich Mitteis unter besonderer Berücksichtigung seines Verhältnisses zum Nationalsozialismus* (Frankfurt, 1991).
[26] See A. W. B. Simpson, *A history of the common law of contract. The rise of the action of assumpsit* (Oxford, 1975); P. S. Atiyah, *The rise and fall of freedom of contract* (Oxford, 1979); M. Lobban, *The common law and English jurisprudence 1760–1850* (Oxford, 1991).

Frank and Eckhardt. Their short biographies were followed by
an attempt to understand their motives.

Hans Fehr (1874–1961) was a Swiss legal historian who studied mainly in Germany and taught there for several years before
ending his career in Bern (1924–44). He studied legal history
in Berlin under such famous masters as Heinrich Brunner and
Otto von Gierke and obtained his *Habilitation* in Leipzig under Rudolf Sohm, which led to professorships in Jena, Halle,
Heidelberg and, finally, Bern, in his home country.

Although a pupil of great classical authors, he went his own
innovative way. Instead of merely following the traditional path
of presenting the development of German private and public law along positivist lines, he directed his research towards
legal ethnology and archaeology, publishing books on law in
German folk-song, law and legend, law in pictorial representations and law in poetry (the author was himself a gifted painter).
All these interests stemmed from his belief that law was but one
of the manifestations of the *Volksgeist* and from his enthusiasm
for the historic Germany, following Johann Gottfried Herder
and Jakob Grimm. He cast his net so wide that he incurred criticism for shallowness and insufficient mastery of the numerous
disciplines he was working in. Nevertheless his *Deutsche Rechtsgeschichte*, based on lectures given during the First World War, was
popular and, between 1921 and 1962, went through six editions.

During his years in Germany and even after his return home
Fehr followed with interest political events under Wilhelm II,
Weimar and the Third Reich. He believed in German culture
and German greatness and consequently had some sympathy
with certain policies of the German government after 1933, but
was repelled by its authoritarianism, as one might expect from a
Swiss citizen. His belief in the people – and not the jurists trained
in the Pandects – as the true source of true law happened to be
in unison with the feeling of the NSDAP. In medieval times, we
read in his *Deutsche Rechtsgeschichte*, law was in accordance with
the *Volksgeist* and 'part of the great process of life'. However,
since the *Rezeption* 'German law, which was full of life', was being

driven out by the learned jurists and 'the great rape of German law took place'. In the same vein he wrote that 'the value of a person was rooted in the nation, as was the value of the law and of the state'. In 1943 Fehr described the fruit of the National Socialist state as 'a newly born natural law' (a truly extraordinary statement), where centre stage was occupied, not by the individual but by the people, 'the social body . . . built on blood, soil and intellectual activity'. This nature-given greatness 'was absolute and eternal . . . and only to be fathomed through the study of history'.[27] This sort of well-worn tirade must have been sweet music to the ears of the masters of the Third Reich, but Fehr never went so far as to give the regime his express support. In the 1943 edition of his *Deutsche Rechtsgeschichte*, in a chapter on the 'National Socialist Reich', he showed understanding of the impact of the humiliating Treaty of Versailles and of the misrule of the political parties and unemployment on the political scene of the thirties, and described the National Socialist renovation of the Reich as the rise of a 'total state', 'in full movement', but for the rest limited himself to a few neutral remarks on the *Führerprinzip* and other Nazi doctrines, none of which amounted to an outright endorsement of the new regime.[28]

Hans Erich Feine (1890–1965) was for many years Professor of German Law and Ecclesiastical Law in the university of Tübingen. In international circles of legal historians he was mainly famous for his *History of the law of the Catholic Church*.[29] It is a comprehensive and authoritative work, based on the pioneering research of his teacher in Berlin, Ulrich Stutz, and a masterly survey of almost 2,000 years of the constitutional history of the

---

[27] See J. Rückert, 'Der Rechtsbegriff der Deutschen Rechtsgeschichte in der NS-Zeit', in Rückert and Willoweit (eds.), *Die Deutsche Rechtsgeschichte*, 209–10.

[28] See on all this E. Wadle, 'Visionen vom "Reich". Streiflichter zur Deutschen Rechtsgeschichte zwischen 1933 und 1945', in Rückert and Willoweit (eds.), *Die Deutsche Rechtsgeschichte*, 286–7. A brief notice on Hans Fehr was published by A. Erler in *Deutsches Rechtswörterbuch* I (Berlin, 1971), 1093–4 and an 'In memoriam Hans Fehr' by K. S. Bader appeared in the *Zeitschrift der Savigny-Stiftung für Rechtsgeschichte*, G.A. 80 (1963), xv–xxxviii.

[29] *Kirchliche Rechtsgeschichte. Die Katholische Kirche*, which appeared in a fifth edition in 1972.

Roman Church. The author, who was a Protestant, wrote in a scholarly and ecumenical spirit which was universally praised.

In an earlier phase, however, he had worked on the constitution of the German empire in modern times, and especially the appointment of bishops in the old Reich. This interest in public law led to important work on the constitutional and political history of his country. He regretted its ancient internal divisions and hoped for a strong and unified nation state. This, and his bitter disappointment at Germany's defeat in the First World War, led him to have some sympathy for the Nazi movement and its programme of national renovation. The result was a schizophrenic predicament where a convinced Christian and practising Protestant (who supported his bishop against Nazi encroachment and strongly rejected racism) could express his admiration for the Third Reich as the fulfilment of German history. In the very year of the appointment of Adolf Hitler as chancellor Feine published an address entitled 'National Socialist political reconstruction and German history'.[30] He praised, *inter alia*, the end of parliamentarism and the multi-party state, and the elimination of the autonomy of the Länder by the new unitary Reich and concluded with the nostalgic wish that 'God should not refuse the German people the realization of its deepest wish, to found for all those who wanted to join it a great Holy empire of the German Nation'.[31] In a book of 1936 the author, in the same vein, praised the role of the National Socialist revolution and the *Führergedanke* in the realization of the old German dream of political greatness.[32]

Feine's national pride even caused him to date a book that happened to come out in the summer of 1940 with the boastful

---

[30] 'Nationalsozialistischer Staatsumbau und Deutsche Geschichte', *Deutschland in der Wende der Zeiten. Öffentliche Vorträge der Universität Tübingen* II (Stuttgart, Berlin, 1933), 203–26.

[31] The word 'Roman' was dropped from the ancient name of *das Heilige Römische Reich Deutscher Nation*.

[32] *Das Werden des deutschen Staates seit dem Ausgang des Heiligen Römischen Reichs, 1800 bis 1933. Eine verfassungsgeschichtliche Darstellung* (Stuttgart, 1936). See on all this Wadle, 'Visionen vom "Reich"', 261–5.

words 'published on the day of the entry of the German army in Paris',[33] a gesture that led to his removal, in May 1946, from the university of Tübingen by a decision of the French Governor (the city was in the French zone of occupation; he was reinstated in 1955).[34]

Claudius Freiherr von Schwerin (1880–1944) was one of the leading German legal historians of the first half of the twentieth century. He worked in the tradition of Karl von Amira, whose pupil he was, and Heinrich Brunner, whose authoritative *Deutsche Rechtsgeschichte* he published in a second, revised edition in 1928. He edited lawbooks of the early and of the later Middle Ages and published detailed studies on various aspects of medieval Germanic, Scandinavian and German private and public law. Von Schwerin taught, *inter alia*, in Freiburg and Munich and was a member of numerous academies and learned societies in Germany and abroad.

Claudius von Schwerin was born in Passau, Bavaria, to an old aristocratic and Catholic family which had lost its privileges at the beginning and its landed wealth around the middle of the nineteenth century. The family produced numerous magistrates. As a student in Munich von Schwerin was impressed by Karl von Amira, a specialist in ancient Germanic, particularly Scandinavian, law, and he decided early to follow in his master's footsteps and become a historian. He eventually succeeded to his teacher's chair in Munich in 1935. He died in 1944 in a bombing raid on that city.[35]

Having grown up in Wilhelmine Germany and in conservative monarchist surroundings, he was shocked by the proclamation of the Weimar Republic. Although he became *professor*

---

33 The book concerned was the second edition of his *Deutsche Verfassungsgeschichte der Neuzeit.*
34 See the 'In memoriam Feine' by K. S. Bader in *Zeitschrift der Savigny-Stiftung für Rechtsgeschichte*, 86, *K. A.* 51 (1965), xi–xxxi, and the memoir on Feine by M. Heckel in F. Elsener (ed.), *Lebensbilder zur Geschichte der Tübinger Juristenfakultät* (Tübingen, 1977), 189–213.
35 Our main source of information is W. Simon, *Claudius Freiherr von Schwerin. Rechtshistoriker während dreier Epochen deutscher Geschichte* (Frankfurt, 1991).

ordinarius at Freiburg in the very year of the proclamation of the Weimar Constitution 1919 and happily conducted his teaching and research in the twenties, he found the new regime distasteful. He rejected its parliamentary constitution with its bickering parties and disliked the divisive, democratic tone of the republic, which he accused of weakening the country and destroying the old unity and community sense of the German nation. He nostalgically turned to the era of the ancient Germanic nations and of medieval Germany, where he found the qualities which his own epoch sorely missed, i.e. good faith, loyalty, honour, unity, community feeling and dedication to a great leader. He dreamt of a new, strong Germany, that would rise from the ashes of the First World War and the humiliation of Versailles. The law of this new Germany would be based on authentic Germanic sources and not on foreign imports. His inaugural lecture at Freiburg, on 4 July 1921, was significantly entitled 'Germanic and foreign law'. It was in this line of thought that he published his *Introduction to the study of Germanic legal history* in 1922 and his *Germanic legal history* in 1936.[36]

Von Schwerin's veneration for all things Germanic, his German patriotism and his aversion to the Weimar Republic were obviously in accordance with several basic ideas of the National Socialist party. It is therefore interesting to see how he reacted to the 'legal Revolution' that brought it to power in 1933. Baron von Schwerin certainly did not throw himself headlong into politics, but carried on lecturing, writing, teaching and examining his students. Nevertheless, his sympathy for the 'national renovation', promised by the new regime, led him to manifest his feelings in no uncertain terms. Already in the fateful year 1933 he joined the *Akademie für Deutsches Recht* founded by Dr Hans Frank (about whom more later), the aim of which was to replace the Civil Code of 1900 by a new *Volksgesetzbuch* (which we mentioned earlier). In 1934 he became a member of the League of National Socialist German

---

[36] *Einführung in das Studium der germanischen Rechtsgeschichte und ihrer Teilgebiete* (Freiburg, 1922); *Germanische Rechtsgeschichte* (Berlin, 1936).

Jurists and in 1938 a member of the National Socialist party. In various addresses and publications he expressed admiration for the *Führerstaat*: already in a lecture of 1932 he explained that a specific Germanic quality allowed the individual 'to give himself up to the Führer and to sacrifice his own ego: to consider this true freedom was the real meaning of loyalty'.[37] In 1934 von Schwerin published his *Grundzüge der deutschen Rechtsgeschichte*, in Munich and Leipzig, which dealt, *inter alia*, with the most recent developments in his country. The author saw the 'national uplift' as the start of a new epoch and praised the combination of the national and the social element, realized by the new regime, as born from 'truly Germanic feeling': the un-Germanic opposition between state and individual had been overcome. What had happened was the 'acceptance of the Germanic Führer idea, based on obedient loyalty (*Treue und Gefolgschaft*), as the cornerstone of the National Socialist state'.[38] In the same year, 1934, von Schwerin also gave a lecture in Freiburg entitled 'The historical foundations of National Socialist law'.[39]

Freiherr von Schwerin resented foreign influence on German law. His ideal was strikingly formulated in his *Grundzüge* of 1934, where he explained that thanks to the new regime 'for the first time since the law of the German territories was created by means of comprehensive legislation, the latter is supported by the unconditional will to give the German people a German law'.[40]

That German law had suffered from foreign contamination but would revive had already been the theme of a contribution by von Schwerin in 1926. It was published in a volume called *Germanic resurrection. A book on the Germanic foundation of our culture* under the title *The spirit of ancient Germanic law, the penetration of*

---

[37] C. von Schwerin, *Freiheit und Gebundenheit im germanischen Staat* (Tübingen, 1933, Recht und Staat in Geschichte und Gegenwart, 99), 19.

[38] See on all this Wadle, 'Visionen vom "Reich"', 279.

[39] The text of the lecture is lost. See Simon, *Claudius Freiherr von Schwerin*, 134.

[40] 'Preface', p. viii. See the comments in Wadle, 'Visionen Vom "Reich"', 279 and n. 58.

foreign law and the recent reinforcement of Germanic legal principles.[41] The culprit was, of course, Roman law, which had changed the normal lines of German development from the sixteenth century until the Pandectist *Bürgerliches Gesetzbuch* four centuries later. Here von Schwerin joined the rejection of 'materialistic' Roman law and the demand for a new community-oriented 'people's law', as formulated in art. 19 of the NSDAP programme (already mentioned). In an essay of 1933 Baron von Schwerin argued, in line with art. 19, that Roman law stood for individualism and materialism ('market values', we might say today, as against 'community values'), which had slowly reduced the Germanic collective sense and consequently had changed German life completely.[42] Small wonder that von Schwerin had, in 1919, called the *Rezeption* a 'violation of German law', and, in 1930, repeated Heinrich Brunner's condemnation of the Pandectist influence on the Civil Code of 1900 as 'a national disaster' because it 'mean-spiritedly ignored German law, and pressed in a mindless and external way Roman norms into native reality', forgetting 'that no nation is capable of thinking with the soul of another'.[43]

Scholars who defended Roman law were given short shrift. Thus E. Schönbauer tried, at a conference in Tübingen in 1936, to save the reputation of Roman law by attributing to it all the qualities traditionally ascribed to Germanic and German law (he even pointed out that the Romans were Aryans). This was going too far for von Schwerin, who insisted that the Germanic

---

[41] H. Nollau (ed.), *Germanische Wiedererstehung: ein Werk über die germanischen Grundlagen unserer Gesittung* (Heidelberg, 1926); Von Schwerin, *Der Geist des altgermanischen Rechts, das Eindringen fremden Rechts, und die neuerliche Wiedererstarkung germanischer Rechtsgrundsätze* (Heidelberg, 1926). See D. Klippel, 'Subjektives Recht und germanisch-deutscher Rechtsgedanke in der Zeit des Nationalsozialismus', in Rückert and Willoweit (eds.), *Deutsche Rechtsgeschichte*, 44 and J. Rückert, 'Der Rechtsbegriff der deutschen Rechtsgeschichte in der NS-Zeit', in *Ibid.*, 208.

[42] *Freiheit und Gebundenheit im germanischen Staat*; cf. Simon, *Claudius Freiherr von Schwerin*, 101.

[43] Thus H. Brunner in his *Grundzüge der deutschen Rechtsgeschichte* (3rd edn, Munich, Leipzig, 1912), 265, repeated in the 8th edn. by C. von Schwerin (Munich, Leipzig, 1930), 264; see Klippel, 'Subjektives Recht', 44–5.

tradition 'was self-sufficient' and that trying to detect in Roman law certain fundamental Germanic notions could only lead to confusion.[44] It should be noted that von Schwerin had not waited till 1933 to form his negative conclusions. Already in his inaugural lecture in Freiburg in 1921 he had spoken of 'Germanic and foreign law', a theme to which he would often return. In his 1921 lecture he criticized the Civil Code of 1900 for being too Romanist and he felt that the rules of German origin preserved in the Code lacked inner ethical and social content, so that 'tribute had been paid to the materialism of the time'.[45]

Although von Schwerin clearly went along with the new rulers, he was more like a fellow-traveller than a hard-bitten fully-fledged party man. This appears, *inter alia*, from his attitude to Erika Sinauer, his Jewish collaborator in the Institute of Legal History at the university of Freiburg for some twenty years. Dr Sinauer was born in Freiburg in 1898, the daughter of a barrister. She studied law in her home town and in the early 1920s became an assistant to Professor von Schwerin, with whom she worked on a critical edition of the Mirror of the Saxons, a thirteenth-century lawbook, and its gloss, for the *Monumenta Germaniae Historica*. As soon as they came to power, the Nazis embarked on a policy of barring Jewish people from teaching and research, and campaigned against all forms of friendship and collaboration between Germans and Jews. In spite of all this, von Schwerin, who had no racist feeling, kept Erika Sinauer on his staff in Freiburg and, after his transfer to Munich, went on supporting her research in Freiburg. This situation, which must have upset the Nazi bosses, lasted until the end of 1938, when a new edict of the Reichsminister for Science, Education and Popular Culture made further employment of Jewish scholars impossible (Erika Sinauer was arrested in 1940 and in 1942 sent to Auschwitz).[46] It is probable that von Schwerin's support

---

[44] Stolleis, *Recht im Unrecht*, 79.
[45] Simon, *Claudius Freiherr von Schwerin*, 109–10.
[46] *Ibid.*, 199–205.

for Dr Sinauer (and the fact that he did not engage in any anti-semitic polemic in his writings) explains the American incident of 1938. In that year an invitation extended to von Schwerin to lecture at Columbia University in New York was vetoed for political reasons. The decision was, *inter alia*, justified in two letters from the legal historian's own university of Munich, sent to the government in Berlin which had asked for information. One came from the Rector and the other from the professorial body. The Rector's letter referred to the position taken by the Dean of the Law Faculty, i.e. that 'in spite of Professor von Schwerin's eminent scholarly qualification certain political reservations existed', which militated against his going to New York. This sharp condemnation was, however, somewhat softened by the – contradictory – statement that von Schwerin was not so much politically unreliable (the term 'politically incorrect' was not yet in use), as having a difficult character, 'which worked as a troublesome rather than a unifying and connecting factor' (was this a coded way of saying that he did not toe the party line?). The letter from the leader of the professorial body was, by contrast, brief and unequivocal, as it stated that the planned American trip should be forbidden because 'Professor von Schwerin does not seem suitable, from a political point of view, to represent Germany abroad in a dignified way'.[47] It is clear that the professor's sympathy for the Nazis was neither unlimited nor unconditional.

Hans Frank (1900–46) was born in Karlsruhe, the son of a barrister. He obtained his doctorate in law in 1924 at the university of Kiel and, in 1927, established himself in Munich as a barrister and lecturer at the local Technical High School. By that time he had been involved in nationalist politics for several years: in 1919–20 he served on the *Freikorps* of Major General Franz Ritter von Epp, which fought the short-lived bolshevik republic in Munich. Around the same time he became a member of the Nordic Thule Society and joined Anton Drexler's

[47] *Ibid.*, 160–1.

German Workers' Party, the forerunner of the NSDAP, of which Frank became a member in 1923, joining at the same time the SA, the party army. On 9 November of the same year he took part in the abortive putsch at the Felherrnhalle in Munich: he was, in other words, an early and active member of Hitler's party. Between 1927 and 1933, when the NSDAP was in the doldrums and taken seriously by very few people, Frank supported the movement by defending party members who had broken the law: some 2,400 cases have been traced. His formal entry into national politics took place in October 1930, when he became a member of the Reichstag, but his great moment came in 1933, when his party took power and Adolf Hitler, whom he worshipped, began to rule Germany.

The rewards for his services to the party were not slow to follow. In 1934 Hans Frank became a Reichsminister without portfolio and leader of the German lawyers with the title of *Reichsjuristenführer*. The *Akademie für Deutsches Recht*, of which Dr Frank became president, was founded as early as 1933. This was to be his most important task in those pre-war years: the reform of German law in the light of the new ideology was a task he took very much to heart, being both a practising and an academic lawyer. The Academy was a learned society, counting 300 members selected for their academic eminence and working in specialized committees. One of its main mandates became the elaboration of the *Volksgesetzbuch* we mentioned earlier.[48]

In the course of these years Dr Frank published several studies and made innumerable speeches about the renovation of German law under the aegis of the Führer. His great source of inspiration was the native Germanic tradition, and he naturally saw Roman law as an alien intruder. This theme we have heard before, but what distinguished him from the three previous jurists was his virulent antisemitism, in which he showed himself a true Nazi. His basic approach was strikingly expressed in the first

[48] Our main source of information is Schudnagies, *Hans Frank*.

issue of the periodical published by his Academy, under the title 'National Socialism and the law'. He wrote: 'We must abandon radically the old way of viewing the law as an end in itself. In the National Socialist state the law can never be anything but a means to maintain, safeguard and enhance the community based on race and people (*rassisch-völkische Gemeinschaft*).'[49]

Frank's insistence on the vital role of the true German tradition led him to expose, as had many others before him, the nefarious consequences of the *Rezeption* of Roman law, which he called 'formalistic'. He rejected the 'so-called Roman law' of the 'glossators, post-glossators, the *usus modernus*, the *codex* and the *novellae* of the Faculties and the doctors of law'; the nineteenth-century pandectists, of course, took their share of the blame. In contrast to this 'formalistic' approach he found, in medieval German law, the 'law of life', i.e. 'peace, freedom and loyalty to the leader' (thus, for example, the 'German spirit' of Eike von Repgow's thirteenth-century 'Mirror of the Saxons').[50] It is in this vein that Dr Frank, who was not averse to rhetorical effects, came to express the extraordinary view that 'between Eike von Repgow and Adolf Hitler the law had been in a state of crisis'.[51]

As a true Nazi Hans Frank could not avoid condemning the Jewish influence on German law. In brutal language worthy of Hitler himself, he maintained that the 'right to life' of the *Volk* justified measures against Jewish lawyers. Frank expressed himself most clearly on this point in a speech to university lecturers on 3 October 1936, in which he opposed the 'realizations of the German spirit' to 'Jewish corruption', and appealed to them to 'banish Jewish jurists and their works from the court

---

[49] *Zeitschrift der Akademie für Deutsches Recht* 1 (1934), 8, quoted by D. Willoweit, 'Deutsche Rechtsgeschichte und "nationalsozialistische Weltanschauung"': das Beispiel Hans Frank', in Stolleis and Simon (eds.), *Rechtsgeschichte im Nationalsozialismus*, 27.

[50] On the notion of *Lebensrecht*, in which 'law, legislation and the state are directly based on life', see Rückert, 'Der Rechtsbegriff der Deutschen Rechtsgeschichte der NS-Zeit', 178.

[51] *Deutsche Rechtspflege* (1938), 283, quoted by Willoweit, 'Deutsche Rechtsgeschichte', 31.

practice and the legal tradition in Germany'.[52] Elsewhere he spoke of the 'legal soul', which belonged to the German people, whereas the Jews had a commercial approach to the law; they were 'abortionists' and 'bastards of the law, and therefore to be eliminated from legal practice and science'.[53]

Frank published, *inter alia*, a 'National Socialist handbook for law and legislation' in Munich in 1935 and in the same year started a new periodical, called *Deutsche Rechtswissenschaft*. It was to combat sceptics, critics and enemies of National Socialism among lawyers (the first issue appeared in 1936).

As Reichsminister Frank invited a group of university professors to draft a set of 'directives on the position and the role of judges' in the light of the new ideology[54] and he invited Professor Karl August Eckhardt (a convinced Nazi, about whom more later) to form a team of young lecturers in order to find 'in comradely collaboration a clear link in the struggle for a German legal science in the National Socialist spirit'. They were told that their only option was 'uncompromising Nazi ideology and a combative attitude' and that 'the surest road . . . went through SA and SS'. The team was to be based at the university of Kiel, whose rector boasted in 1940 that practically all non-Nazi staff had been eliminated and the university, as he put it, 'completely renovated'.[55]

Until the beginning of the Second World War Hans Frank's role had certainly been important, but his influence was limited to the legal arena and he had never been admitted to the inner circle of decision-makers. At no time was he in the eye of the political cyclone. His position as Reichsminister without portfolio was politically irrelevant and the job of Minister of Justice of the Third Reich had eluded him. Academically he may have

---

[52] *Deutsches Recht* (1936), 393 ff., quoted by Willoweit, 'Deutsche Rechtsgeschichte', 29.
[53] *Deutsche Rechtspflege* (1938), 285, quoted by Willoweit, 'Deutsche Rechtsgeschichte', 34.
[54] B. Rüthers, *Entartetes Recht. Rechtslehren und Kronjuristen im Dritten Reich* (Munich, 1994), 21 and 48.
[55] *Ibid.*, 42.

been a heavyweight, but politically he definitely was not: a statesmanlike post, where he could command and issue laws and ordinances, had not come his way. All this changed dramatically in September 1939. Disgruntled with his marginal role in German politics, Hans Frank joined the army and was ready to take part, as a lieutenant, in the Polish campaign when he was summoned, out of the blue, to appear on 15 September 1939 at Headquarters, where Hitler told him that he was to become head of the German civil administration in occupied Poland. At first he was attached to the military commander, General von Rundstedt, but from 26 October onwards he was the independent Governor General of the Generalgouvernement (as the German-occupied part of Poland was to be known). Frank's objection that he would prefer to stay with his Infantry Regiment was brushed aside. His appointment specified that he would be the direct representative of the Führer and responsible only to him.

We can only speculate as to what had moved Hitler to appoint the reluctant president of the Academy for German Law to this far from academic post. Frank was one of his earliest and most loyal 'old comrades' and deserved a position of some importance. And although Hitler had studiously kept this author of legal treatises out of the political limelight in Germany, he may have deemed him good enough to become a German viceroy of 'rump Poland' (a territory ripe for 'colonial and imperial' treatment, to use Frank's own words). Frank went to live in great style in the ancient royal Palace of Cracow. He behaved as a heartless satrap, oppressing and exploiting the conquered nation and issuing numerous laws and decrees which carried the death penalty even for minor offences. He was not personally involved in the extermination camps, which were engineered directly from Berlin by Himmler, the SS and the security police (with whom he quarrelled all the time), but he repeatedly issued antisemitic decrees, gave vent to his racist feelings and called for the annihilation of the Jews (as appears from the Nazi Conspiracy and Aggression Papers, produced at the Nuremberg trial). In January 1945, at the approach of the Red Army, Frank fled to Bavaria where he was arrested in May 1945 by an American lieutenant. He stood trial in Nuremberg (where his forty-two-volume journal was produced as evidence) together with other leading figures of the Third Reich, and was condemned to death for his part in the terror in Poland and executed in the night of 15 to 16 October 1946. He had confessed his guilt and expressed deep regret for what he had done.

So far the reader might form the impression that Hans Frank was a fanatical Nazi and Hitler devotee, who abjured his legal training and forgot all about the principles he had learned. In fact, this was not the case. In a curious way Frank remained attached to the rule of law, even while he was misbehaving in Poland – an amazing phenomenon to which we shall now turn our attention. The advocacy of the *Rechtsstaat*, the law-based state, was over many years a leitmotiv in Frank's speeches and writings. In the very first months of the new regime, he and others hoped that a 'national *Rechtsstaat*' would be founded. In the *Deutsche Verwaltung* of 1934 Hans Frank declared: 'The State of Adolf Hitler is a *Rechtsstaat*', a pronouncement which led to a lively debate among lawyers, some of whom wanted to maintain certain legal safeguards, whilst others condemned that attitude as a relic of the liberalism of the past.[56] In the same year, Frank praised the 'eternal German law' and proclaimed that it should regain the proud characteristics of Germany's great past. In this context he even spoke of 'the constitution' in which the Germans found themselves[57] (constitutional freedoms were anathema to Hitler, who saw to it that the Weimar constitution which had fallen into abeyance was not replaced).

In 1937 the leader of the National Socialist lawyers tried to come to grips with the contradiction between the *Führerstaat*, where one man's will was the law, and the *Rechtsstaat*, where the law, based on the will of the people, was supreme. He talked again of a 'National Socialist constitution' and declared that Hitler was 'the called-for executor of the historic will of the people' (in 1934

[56] Stolleis, *Recht im Unrecht*, 148–9.
[57] Willoweit, 'Deutsche Rechtsgeschichte', 30.

he had said that Hitler had 'restored to the people their legal consciousness and the instinct for their law'). It could be argued that the notion of 'executor' implied that the Führer was not above the law, but had to implement it.[58] Also, the 'will of the people', which Hitler was supposed to execute, was a nebulous concept, which reminds one of the *Volksgeist*, the popular mind which learned jurists such as Savigny were supposed to know best. In the same year 1937 Frank published in the periodical *Deutsches Recht* an article entitled 'Das Recht im Reich', in which he proclaimed that 'every German has his place, even in the law courts, and every German should have his defender everywhere, without any exception and in every lawsuit'.[59] In 1938 Hans Frank gave a lecture in which he proclaimed that the law belonged to the divine order: Germanic and Aryan thought saw the law as the highest form of consciousness, which transformed 'arbitrariness and violence' into a positive attitude towards the community.[60] In 1939 Frank declared that all acts of the administration should be subject to judicial review, which meant that 'administrative courts . . . were even in the National Socialist Reich indispensable'.[61] He, together with other Reichsministers, obtained even Heinrich Himmler's agreement to this point, but only after the leader of the SS had secured legislation to ensure the inviolability of the Gestapo!

In April 1941 Frank became more outspoken in his defence of the *Rechtsstaat*, declaring in an address before the International Chamber of Law, a Nazi satellite organization, that 'an organized state can only last when it satisfies the people: numerous states had been founded on brutality, arbitrariness, violence and tyranny, but none had lasted'.[62] In November 1941, in an address to legal functionaries of the party, he went a step further in his criticism of the police state by mentioning specifically

[58] Whether Frank saw it in that way is doubtful. See *ibid.*, 28.
[59] *Ibid.*, 32.
[60] In *Deutsche Rechtspflege* (1938), 283, quoted in Willoweit, 'Deutsche Rechtsgeschichte', 31.
[61] See his *Recht und Verwaltung* (Munich, 1939), quoted by Stolleis, *Recht im Unrecht*, 194.
[62] Quoted in Willoweit, 'Deutsche Rechtsgeschichte', 32.

that 'by the organization of various police forces an unbearable element of insecurity had entered into the law of the German people'.[63] None of these statements seems to have caused a stir. People, even in the Nazi hierarchy, obviously thought that the president of the Academy for German Law was just riding his old hobby horse again and using the sort of principled language one would expect from a jurist.

In the summer of 1942, however, things changed. While the German army was again progressing deep into Soviet territory, Frank travelled around Germany to give a series of sensational lectures. He addressed a wide public in four renowned universities – Berlin, Vienna, Munich and Heidelberg – and threw himself – to great applause – into a passionate headlong attack on the police state and into an exaltation of the rule of law. This time he addressed, not party officials or fellow academics, but a much broader audience and the public at large. On 9 June 1942 he spoke in Berlin on 'The idea of law and the community of the people' in which he declared: 'a nation cannot be dominated by violence; national life without the law is unthinkable'. On 1 July he spoke in Vienna on 'The law and the renovation of Europe' and declared: 'No Reich without the law – including our own; no law without judges – including German law; no judges without real authority – including German judges!' On 20 July in Munich and on 21 July in Heidelberg he spoke on 'The law as the cornerstone of the community of the people' and on 'The idea of law and the new order in Europe'. On both occasions he was outspoken in his attack on the brutality of the *Polizeistaat* – which should never be allowed – and in his condemnation of contempt for juridical thought and action. This time the Governor General of Poland had gone too far. Hitler curtly dismissed him from his post as President of the Academy for German Law and other leading functions in Germany's legal establishment. He absolutely forbade him to lecture or to publish any more and sent him back to Cracow and eventually, as we have seen, to his doom.

[63] *Ibid.*, 33.

The significance of the four lectures of 1942 is clear. It took courage in the middle of the war to lash out at tyranny in the face of – what was at that time – a victorious tyrant. The lectures also showed that Dr Hans Frank, although a convinced Nazi, continued somehow to believe in the idea of law. There has been a good deal of speculation as to what led him to this sensational step at that particular moment, other than sincere conviction. It has been plausibly argued that his conflicts with the SS and the Gestapo in Poland and their constant encroachments on his authority in the General Government had so exacerbated him that he decided to speak up, in the vain hope that he could reverse certain deplorable trends. It is also just possible that he still had some illusions about Hitler's respect for the 'great principles of Germanic law', although various pronouncements of the Führer, who hated the law, the courts and the lawyers, should have enlightened him long before on that score.[64]

Hans Frank was a gifted intellectual, but over-ambitious and easily carried away by grandiose phrases, including his own. He could rise to the occasion and have the courage of his convictions, but he had no strong personality and was mesmerized by the real men of power. All too often racial pride and blind faith in his leader got the better of his lawyer's instinct. Although he condemned Hitler after 1945, he never stood up to him as long as he was alive – but then very few people did.

Karl August Eckhardt (1901–79) was born in Witzenhausen, in Hessen, on 5 March 1901, the son of a judge in a family of lawyers and clerics. He was one of the most learned legal historians of his century, and especially famous for his editions of medieval lawbooks. He also was a convinced supporter of the Nazi movement and an influential figure in the Ministry of Science under the Third Reich. Perusing his biography one wonders whether his numerous incongruous activities really belonged to one and the same man. The astonished reader asks

---

[64] For a selection of Hitler's terms of abuse ('complete cretins', a 'cancer for the German people') see Rüthers, *Entartetes Recht*, 22. On the lectures of 1942 see Schudnagies, *Hans Frank*, 61–3.

himself: 'am I having a hallucination or were there in fact two
different men with the same name?' And in a sense there were
indeed two Karl August Eckhardts. There was the scholar who
produced, among many other works, critical editions of the *Lex
salica* and the *Sachsenspiegel* and whose total output amounted to
some 30,000 pages in print, but there was also another Karl
August Eckhardt, who became a *Sturmbannführer* in the SS, a
close friend of *Reichsführer* SS Heinrich Himmler, and the author of vapid studies on 'Earthly immortality: Germanic belief
in the re-embodiment in the kin'.[65] The fact remains nevertheless that the medievalist and the SS man were one and the same
person, even though reading about him remains an uncanny
experience. It was, in those circumstances, not surprising that
finding a scholar to write Eckhardt's obituary in the authoritative
Savigny-Zeitschrift für Rechtsgeschichte took a long time. When eventually it came out, in 1987, eight years after Eckhardt's death, the
author, Hermann Nehlsen, explained that few colleagues were
prepared to undertake the task because of Eckhardt's behaviour
in the years 1933–45.[66]

We shall here proceed briefly to outline Eckhardt's curriculum
vitae in the form of two 'parallel lives', even though they concern
one and the same person. We shall first present the learned
jurist and university professor, and then the *Sturmbannführer* and
member of Himmler's *Ahnenerbe* ('Heritage of the Forefathers'),
a research centre for genealogy and the tracing of Jewish and
Aryan ancestry. Afterwards we shall see whether it is possible to
link the two together in a way that makes sense.

Karl August Eckhardt was a brilliant young man who obtained his doctorate in law in Marburg in 1922 with a study
on a medieval German lawbook. Thereafter he studied in the
Faculty of Philosophy at Göttingen, where he became a *Privat-
dozent* in 1924 – not yet twenty-three years old. By 1928 he was

[65] *Irdische Unsterblichkeit. Germanischer Glaube an die Wiederverkörperung in der Sippe* (Weimar, 1937).
[66] H. Nehlsen, 'Karl August Eckhardt', *Zeitschrift der Savigny Stiftung für Rechtsgeschichte* 104 (1987), 497–536. This thorough presentation has been our main source of information.

already a *professor ordinarius* at Kiel, teaching legal history and
civil and commercial law. After a brief spell at a commercial
high school in Berlin he obtained, in 1932, a chair of German
Law and Commercial Law at Bonn. He was a prodigy, who at the
age of thirty-one had already been offered three posts as *professor
ordinarius* and could boast some seventy publications. After a year
as dean of the Bonn Law Faculty he went briefly back to Kiel and,
in 1935, became a professor in the university of Berlin, before
going back, in 1937, to Bonn, where he stayed for the rest of his
university career, occupying the chair of Germanic Legal History, Family Law and Genealogical Research. His main scholarly
attention during those years was on the edition of medieval lawbooks. After the war he was dismissed from his university post
for political reasons (on which more in a moment), granted a
pension and retired to his native town of Witzenhausen. Here
he applied himself with obsessive devotion to the publication of
medieval sources and the creation of series of studies and editions, in such abundance (and with so many revised editions and
reprints) that he drove librarians and bibliographers to despair.[67]
His astounding output assures him of a place among the great
monstra eruditionis of the past, in the company of a Du Cange and
a Theodor Mommsen. Doubtless his most outstanding achievement was the edition in 1962 and 1969 of the Salic Law in the
Monumenta Germaniae Historica. Bringing out this standard edition
was a remarkable achievement because there exist several versions and numerous manuscripts with variants, stretching over
several centuries (the oldest version of the *Lex Salica* probably
dates from the early sixth century). Until Eckhardt, all attempts
at a critical edition of that famous text, which from the start had
been on the programme of the *Monumenta Germaniae Historica*,
had failed. Some great medievalists and legal historians

---

[67] A detailed and systematic bibliography was fortunately provided by one of his sons:
A. Eckhardt (ed.), *Werksverzeichnis Karl August Eckhardt* (Aalen, 1979) (vol. XVII in
K. A. Eckhardt's series *Bibliotheca Rerum Historicarum*). For an account of the con-
nections between Eckhardt's publications, see the obituary notice by H. Krause in
Deutsches Archiv für Erforschung des Mittelalters 35 (1979), 8–16.

(G. H. Pertz, R. Sohm) had given up in despair and one edition, by Mario Krammer, was already in print when a final critical evaluation by a body of experts led to the destruction of all the copies (except one or two which are now museum pieces). Like many of his fellow scholars the retired professor Eckhardt was honoured with a collection of studies on the occasion of his sixtieth birthday. The *Festschrift* contained fourteen articles on town and country history and the preface praised Eckhardt's merits as a local historian (which he was, among many other things, as already by 1925 he had written a history of his native town).[68]

Let us now turn our spotlight on Eckhardt the *Sturmbannführer*. While a student in Marburg young Eckhardt had as a volunteer fought the attempted communist take-over in Thuringia in the spring of 1920, but he showed no further interest in party politics until he, ten years later, became involved with the National Socialist movement in Kiel. It was a speech by Hitler to the Berlin students, in December 1930, which won him over once and for all. In May 1931 he joined the SA, in 1932 he became a member of the party and in October 1933 he joined the SS (he became *Sturmbannführer* in 1938). He soon joined Heinrich Himmler's High Command and became a member of the latter's personal staff. In 1934 he was appointed to a leading administrative position in the Ministry of Science and Education, and launched himself with zeal into the reform of the universities and the renewal of their teaching staffs, all, of course, in line with the new regime. He was responsible for law, politics, economics and history, and as such one of the most powerful figures in the academic world. He was, by the way, instrumental in abolishing the autonomy of the universities – a well-known thorn in the flesh of political masters – and was the author of a 'criminal

---

[68] O. Perst (ed.), *Festschrift zum 60. Geburtstag von Karl August Eckhardt* (Marburg/Lahn and Witzenhausen, 1961, Beiträge zur Geschichte der Werralandschaft, 12). The Preface, which remains completely silent about Eckhardt's political role, explains that several scholars had declined to contribute because of pressure of work, but that they all said how sorry they were and that he deserved this form of literary thanksgiving.

ordinance for students', aimed at disciplining this sometimes un-
ruly segment of the population.

In the meantime his collaboration – and friendship – with
Himmler continued: in 1941 he produced – together with two
SS *Brigadeführer* and other SS officers – a *Festschrift* for him on the
occasion of his fortieth birthday. Along the same lines Eckhardt
became leader of the *Deutschrechtliches Institut des Reichsführers SS*,
a department of Himmler's *Ahnenerbe*.[69]

As a convinced Nazi, Eckhardt was antisemitic.[70] This involved him in the vexed question of how Christians could be
anti-Jewish when Jesus Christ himself was of Jewish origin. To
this issue Eckhardt devoted a long article under the title 'Was
Jesus a Jew?' and, as other antisemitic authors in France and
Germany before him, came to the 'on scientific grounds irre-
proachable conclusion that Jesus was through neither his father
nor his mother of Jewish blood'. Himmler, to whom the author
sent his manuscript in December 1941, was personally interested in the problem, and pleased with the text. He nevertheless
advised against publication in the series of his *Deutschrechtliches
Institut*, at least till after the war, probably out of fear of protest
by the Churches. Eckhardt eventually did publish his paper at
another place and under a different title, i.e. 'The origin of
the Messiah'.[71] Himmler, who had given up his Catholic faith
long ago, dabbled in Germanic pseudo-religious fantasies, even

---

[69] H.-J. Becker, 'Neuheidentum und Rechtsgeschichte', in Rückert and Willoweit (eds.),
Deutsche Rechtsgeschichte in der NS-Zeit, 20.

[70] That Eckhardt had, however, not given up the common decencies of a scholar –
and that there was a good deal of infighting within the Nazi ranks – was shown by
the incident around Professor Max Pappenheim's obituary. Eckhardt had, in 1934,
praised the scholarly achievement and the fine character of his Jewish predecessor
in Kiel and he was said to believe in a distinction between 'bad' and 'good', or
'corrupting' and 'German' Jews. This displeased Hitler so much that he intervened in
the struggle for the appointment of a Director General of the Prussian State Archives.
Hitler decided, in 1937, against Eckhardt because of his unsatisfactory attitude in
the Jewish question, as shown in the Pappenheim obituary. See Nehlsen, 'Eckhardt',
508–9.

[71] 'Die Herkunft des Messias', *Archiv für Religionsgeschichte* 31 (1943), 257–317. See on all
this Nehlsen, 'Eckhardt', 518–19 and Becker, 'Neuheidentum', 15. The article stated
that the author was solely concerned with religious science and did not want to enter
into the theological implications.

dreaming of restoring the cult of Thor and Woden. Eckhardt, who had left his Protestant Church in 1934, was also hooked by these strange metaphysics. He studied ancient Aryan and Germanic ideas on immortality and apparently convinced himself that there was a Germanic sort of reincarnation through the kin – which linked up nicely with the *Ahnenerbe*. His *Irdische Unsterblichkeit* of 1937, which we have already mentioned, very much pleased Himmler, who carried on a lively correspondence with the author. Eckhardt also espoused Himmler's idea that the time had come – or would soon come after German victory – for Germanic neo-paganism to settle accounts with Christianity. He talked of the 'bloody war of extermination waged by the Catholic Churches against the Aryans' and he wrote to Himmler offering to accentuate the anti-Christian arguments in his *Irdische Unsterblichkeit* in a future popular edition.[72]

It is also well known that the SS nurtured a special hatred of homosexuals. Eckhardt, who was interested in Germanic criminal law, praised capital punishment 'which stemmed from the instinct to preserve the purity of the race'. In 1935 he published in the SS periodical *Das Schwarze Korps* an article under the unequivocal title 'Unnatural sex deserves death', in which he argued that according to Tacitus the ancient Germans drowned homosexuals in bogs; and he equated homosexuality with cowardice, explaining in typical Nazi style (with all the familiar bugbears) that this Nordic-Germanic severity had been falsified and weakened by the doctrine of the Christian Church, the French Revolution and the emancipation of the Jews, which entailed the 'danger of a complete corruption of the race'. Everyone knew, the author concluded, that 'Germany stands and falls with the purity of race'[73]. It is clear that Eckhardt believed in all

---

[72] Nehlsen, 'Eckhardt', 520.

[73] *Ibid.*, 516–17. The topic was far from academic. Himmler took severe measures against homosexual SS men: they were to be demoted, handed over to the criminal courts and after undergoing the punishment imposed by them, they were to be sent to a concentration camp and shot 'while attempting to escape'. See on all this Stolleis, 'Fortschritte der Rechtsgeschichte', in Stolleis and Simon (eds.), *Rechtsgeschichte im Nationalsozialismus*, 196.

this: he did not need to publish this sort of writing for the sake of his career for, as a university professor, he had an established position.

When war broke out Eckhardt was drafted into the army. His repeated requests to be transferred to the *Waffen* SS were unsuccessful. This was just as well, for heaven knows in what misdeeds he might otherwise have been involved. Instead, he spent much of the war in Paris, officially serving in Military Intelligence but in fact copying *Lex salica* manuscripts at the *Bibliothèque Nationale*. In 1944 he was made a prisoner of war in Normandy. After the war the Denazification Authorities classed him as a mere party-hack (*Mitläufer*) – which was good for him, if not for his pride – and, as we have seen, he went to live in retirement in Witzenhausen. The contrast with the fate of his fellow-Nazi jurist Hans Frank was striking.

At the start of this presentation we wondered how the two Eckhardts could be reconciled with each other. The problem exists, however, for the other four men also, as they were all learned jurists and in varying degrees involved in Nazi politics or ideology. The moment has come to examine what led these academics to sympathize with the Third Reich. As was predictable, this question provoked a lively discussion among the students. The general sentiment was that Germany's bitter disappointment after the World War led to the exacerbation of national feeling that was common to our jurists. Until November 1918 and the ensuing Treaty of Versailles Germans had believed that the twentieth century would be their century. German science and culture as well as German economic and military strength were universally recognized. Her successful unification had put an end to centuries of division and weakness, so that the empire would at last catch up and even surpass the older nation states of Europe. In 1918 all these high hopes came crashing down: German culture was disparaged, the economy was crippled with war reparations and the monarchy, which had symbolized re-gained glory, was replaced by a republic which, among other things, had signed the humiliating Treaty of Versailles. Wounded pride and even a feeling of despair led to the exaltation of past German greatness and the virtues of the Germanic ancestors. The shock of the events – the flight of the emperor, the proclamation of an unstable republic, various attempted communist take-overs – provoked a nostalgia for the 'good old times'. Many jurists lived in enmity with their own time and invented a past of their dreams to meet the challenge of the awful present.[74] They so desperately hoped for national redemption that their scholarly training and critical sense were overcome by emotion, and there seemed to be no limit to their self-delusion.

The exaltation of the German traditions went hand in hand with aversion to Roman law and alleged Jewish influences. Article 19 of the NSDAP programme was, as we have seen, explicit on this point: Roman law was individualistic and capitalist and a foreign body, which had to give way to the community feeling of the good old German law. Some students expressed surprise at discovering the extraordinary impact of this mythology on the roughly 20,000 participants in the *Deutscher Juristentag* at Leipzig in 1933, who visited an exhibition devoted to 'German law and the struggle against foreign law' and listened to speeches on the learned lawyers' law and the people's law (*Juristenrecht* as opposed to *völkisches Recht*) and against individual fundamental rights.[75]

Legal historians disagree on the importance of the famous art. 19. Koschaker, who devoted a chapter of his book *Europe and Roman law* to the question, minimized its impact on legal policy, and poked fun at popular but ignorant party orators who decried Roman law as the enemy of the peasants before equally ignorant audiences in the countryside, 'who may well have gained the impression that Roman law was some pernicious

---

74 See on this widespread human reaction: E. Hobsbawm and T. Ranger (eds.), *The invention of tradition* (Cambridge, 1992).

75 Leipzig witnessed a torch-lit procession, and heard one particularly insane address on the impact of Nordic man on China and Persia, besides a speech by Hitler and much racist talk. See Landau, 'Die deutschen Juristen und der nationalsozialistische Deutsche Juristentag in Leipzig', 373–90.

sort of foot and mouth disease'; he also made the cynical remark that law students who failed their Roman law exam might have applauded art. 19. Koschaker also pointed out that it had to be understood as one of a series of socialist articles, but he nevertheless found it truly mysterious, because he was at a loss as to its origins.[76] Recent research, by Peter Landau, has solved this riddle and uncovered the forerunners and the author of art. 19.[77] Landau also attaches more importance to the 1920 programme than Koschaker and says that even if art. 19 was not widely understood by the party members, it nevertheless contained representations resulting from the popular view of the legal past, in which he distinguished three elements. Firstly, the existing law, i.e. the Civil Code of 1900, was Roman based, materialistic and therefore to be rejected. Secondly, the German *Gemeinrecht* was extolled because it embodied the idealistic values of the German nation: in spite of the *Rezeption* the conservative tradition of German legal thought was never lost. And thirdly, this tradition implied the existence of a homogeneous nation and needed a legal theory based on folk and race: a 'doctrine according to the law of race' was required.[78]

Gemeinrecht or community law was a loaded term, because of the debate on the merits of community versus society (*Gemeinschaft* as opposed to *Gesellschaft*). The sociologist Tönnies had praised 'community' as a person's organic ties to intimate social life, to family and relatives, to neighbourhoods and friendships, to village and city, as against 'society' with its mechanical relationships shaped by conflicts of interest, contractual relationships and the loss of all ties, loyalties and values.[79] The Middle Ages were idealized – here we meet the nostalgic reflex

---

[76] P. Koschaker, *Europa und das Römische Recht* (Munich, 1947), 312–13.

[77] There is no need here to enter into details and to mention these obscure ideologues and their forgotten writings. The interested reader will find a detailed analysis in Landau, 'Römisches Recht und deutsches Gemeinrecht', 11–24.

[78] The term *rassengesetzliche Rechtslehre* was used by the Nazi legal philosopher Helmut Nicolai in 1932. See Landau, 'Römisches Recht', 12–13.

[79] F. Tönnies had published his *Gemeinschaft und Gesellschaft* in 1887.

again – as the great era of the community, whilst modern society was condemned and consigned to destruction.[80]

Several students felt that the fear of bolshevism was another powerful agent. There is indeed no doubt that western Europe in general and Germany in particular were obsessed with the Soviet Revolution and the abortive bolshevik republics in Hungary, Bavaria and Thuringia. Some of our five jurists had even joined paramilitary groups to fight the communists. It is clear that they, like many others, and not only in Germany, saw Hitler's anti-communist party as a welcome dam against the threat from the East. Other students felt that the decline of the traditional Churches helped to explain the rise of secular religions dedicated to the glorification of race, the reintroduction of the cult of the Germanic gods and other ingredients of the 'Myth of the Twentieth Century'.

That Germans were attached to German law was no problem for the students: after all, the English are proud of their common law and the French of their civil code. But what intrigued them was how twentieth-century Germans raved about the virtues of their Germanic ancestors of two thousand years ago. How could those Teutonic warriors, who kept Roman civilisation out of their forests east of the Rhine, were illiterate heathens, animists and slave-owners and lived in *Grubenhäuser* (half-sunken huts), be a source of inspiration for the subjects of Wilhelm II? They admittedly overran the western Roman empire and founded Germanic kingdoms in Gaul, Britain, Italy and Spain, and they produced Charlemagne, one of the most eminent monarchs of European history, whose mother tongue was Frankish, a West Germanic language. Also, Tacitus had lauded their personal virtues and their free institutions, but was his *Germania* not in

---

[80] See O. G. Oexle, 'The Middle Ages through modern eyes. A historical problem', *Transactions of the Royal Historical Society*, sixth series, 9 (1999), 131. The author believes that the foundation for these concepts was laid by the German Romantics, namely the poet Novalis in his speech 'Die Christenheit oder Europa', of 1799, which celebrated the Middle Ages as an epoch of wholeness, unity and community. Novalis was the pseudonym of Friedrich Leopold Freiherr von Hardenberg (1772–1801).

fact a veiled attack on the corruption of his own society rather than an exact description of reality? In any case it remained a mystery how the rustic tribal law of Clovis (Chlodovech, the 'illustrious fighter') and his primitive farmers and cattle-holders could be a source of pride and inspiration for the industrialized German empire.

It soon became obvious that the explanation was to be found in the projection of present-day concerns on to a mythological past. Moreover, this Teutonic enthusiasm was in no way limited to Germany, but was shared by Anglo-American historians and lawyers and even by Frenchmen like Montesquieu, who extolled the achievements of the ancient Germans and maintained that they were the ancestors of the French nobility, the mass of their subject peasants being descended from the conquered natives of Gaul.

An early English spokesman of this Germanism was Henry Spelman, a graduate of Trinity College, Cambridge, a student at Lincoln's Inn and a member of the Society of Antiquaries in London, where he pursued a life of scholarship and published, *inter alia*, a dictionary of medieval legal terminology, called the *Archaeologus*. In 1635 he endowed a readership at Cambridge to promote the study of Anglo-Saxon. Spelman believed that the common law was rooted in the Anglo-Saxon past, so that it ultimately went back to the ancient Germans, whom he called 'a prime and most potent people'.[81]

The next famous defender of the Teutonic forests was Bishop William Stubbs, Regius Professor of Modern History at Oxford from 1866 to 1884, when he became a bishop, first of Chester and then of Oxford. He believed in the 'Germanic roots of Anglo-American freedom', as we explained above (p. 97).[82] Being a true *érudit* did not stop Bishop Stubbs having strong

---

[81] D. R. Kelley, 'History, English law and the Renaissance', *Past and Present* 65 (1974), 48.

[82] I borrow the phrase from the subtitle of a recent study by Reimann, '"In such forests liberty was nurtured". Von den germanischen Wurzeln der anglo-amerikanischen Freiheit'.

prejudices: he liked the Germans and 'could not bear the French', calling them 'liars'.[83]

Stubbs's Germanic path had been prepared by lesser scholars: in 1849 John Mitchell Kemble, who had studied under Jacob Grimm, published in London a work in two volumes entitled *The Saxons in England*, in which he stressed the Germanic character of the conquerors of Roman Britain.

Historical myths are untrue but useful, and the Germanist myth was a mode of rationalizing the juristic and political desire of the time. It more specifically served to combat Romanism, both in the political and the religious field. To Bishop Stubbs Rome stood for the Catholic Church, popery, intolerance and a threat to the liberal Anglican tradition. Stubbs was not only pleased that the Church of which he was a bishop had, ever since the Reformation, been free from papal control, he went a step further and believed that even before the sixteenth century the English Church had, as Richardson and Sayles put it, 'successfully resisted all attempts by the mediaeval papacy to encroach upon its primitive and native authority'.[84]

However, the Oxford medievalist went too far in the projection of his concerns on the distant past. His thesis was refuted by W. F. Maitland, who showed that the medieval English Church had lived under the universal authority and legislation of Rome, as did everyone else in the Latin West.[85] As Richardson and Sayles again put it: 'He projected his bias into the Middle Ages and, interpreting the evidence in the light of a cherished doctrine, he failed to see the real problem.'[86] To the common lawyers, who in this respect were on the same wavelength, Roman law stood for absolutism, slavery and foreign interference. They knew that in the struggles of the seventeenth century, their predecessors defended Parliament, whereas the

[83] See his collection of letters, quoted by H. G. Richardson and G. O. Sayles, *The governance of mediaeval England from the Conquest to Magna Carta* (Edinburgh, 1963), 4–5.
[84] *Ibid.*, 19.
[85] See on this famous controversy: *Ibid.*, 9–12.
[86] *Ibid.*, 12.

civilians inclined in the other direction. The Elizabethan lawyer and antiquary William Lambarde praised the common law as 'standing upon the highest reason selected even for itself' and added that 'English law was like a wall built of stone and oak to defend a city'.[87] Absolutism inspired by imperial Rome was the enemy that threatened the English 'city' and its defender, the common law. More than three centuries later, but in a similar vein, Roscoe Pound, of the Harvard Law School, viewed the history of the common law as a series of victories over successive attacks launched by Roman law, both in its secular and its ecclesiastical guise.[88] As he put it, in anthropomorphic imagery, 'the common law has passed triumphantly through more than one crisis in which it seemed that an alien system might supersede it; it has contended with more than one powerful antagonist and has come forth victor'.[89] Pound then proceeded to name the repulsed enemies of the common law. In the twelfth century it was the Church, 'the strongest force of that time'. In the sixteenth century, 'when the Roman law was sweeping over Europe', the common law stood firm. In the seventeenth, the common law 'contended with the English crown'. In America, after the Revolution, it 'prevailed over the prejudice against all things English, which for a time threatened a reception of French law' (even here the civilian danger was not far away). And the author concluded, with obvious relief, that 'the triumph of the common law' seemed secure, even though – he warned the reader – this was only 'superficially' so, as 'at the very moment of triumph' a new crisis was at hand (but that is another story that need not detain us here).[90] The English lawyer and legal historian Frederick Pollock had not felt differently when he wrote that the 'homegrown stock of legal institutions . . . grew up in rugged

[87] Kelley, 'History, English law and the Renaissance', 37.
[88] Already in the fourteenth century John Wycliffe, in his *De officio regis*, had asserted the sufficiency of English case law against the venerable legislation of Justinian and the sacred decretals of the popes: R. Pound, *The spirit of the common law* (Boston, 1921), 39.
[89] *Ibid.*, 5.
[90] *Ibid.*, 5–6.

exclusiveness disdaining fellowship with the more polished learning of the civilians, and it was well that they did so'.[91] Nearer to our time, the Cambridge legal historian John Baker stressed that although the common law was aware of continental models, it withstood 'two waves of Romanist influence which swept across the Continent' and was immunized against any 'fatal infection' by the civil law because early royal judges had been in touch with the new learning from Bologna.[92] In Germany also, as we have seen, Roman law stood for slavery and betrayal of hallowed native values.

But it is time to conclude this exercise in deconstruction. Clearly, when the Germanists extolled the old Nordic values, they were saying that their Teutonic ancestors – who, after all, had beaten the Romans both in Britain and on the Continent – were as ancient and noble as the Mediterranean nations that produced the *Corpus iuris*. There was therefore no reason why they should give up their native laws – or their national Churches – in favour of foreign imports.[93]

---

[91] In his *English opportunities in historical and comparative jurisprudence* of 1890, quoted by M. Reimann, '*Who is afraid of the civil law?* Kontinentaleuropäisches Recht und Common Law im Spiegel der englischen Literatur seit 1500', *Zeitschrift für Neuere Rechtsgeschichte* 21 (1999), 372.

[92] J. Baker, *An introduction to English legal history* (3rd edn, London, 1990), 33. The Romanist spook haunted not only the legal but also the artistic world: in 1850 John Ruskin attacked the painter J. E. Millais for his 'Romanism', referring to a Catholic-inspired religious feeling.

[93] Reimann, 'In such forests', speaks of a conscious or unconscious 'international alliance' of German and English Germanists in the struggle against the predominance of Roman law.

Epilogue: A look into the twenty-first century[1]

That external factors have an impact on the law is obvious enough: we have studied in some detail how the cultural climate in twelfth-century Europe led to the rebirth of ancient Roman jurisprudence and how, in nineteenth- and twentieth-century Germany, political concerns and patriotic passion were focused on the Civil Code. It would, however, be a mistake to underrate the internal logic that operates within legal systems and determines their progress independently of cultural fashion or political pressure. Generations of civilians distilled their concepts and norms from authoritative premises by applying the rules of logic. Thus we can trace the continuous refinement of the notion of tort through a span of more than two thousand years, from the *Lex aquilia* to art. 1382 of the *Code civil*. Similarly, English judges patiently formulated, in the course of many centuries, certain fundamental norms on the strength of precedents and *obiter dicta* handed down by their predecessors; those judges applied the eternal equitable and reasonable principles of the common law to the cases before them, irrespective of the commotions and upheavals that raged outside the sacred halls of their courts.

Whether external events or internal logic is more important for the development of the law is a moot point. It reminds us of the discussion that separates the 'reductionists' from the 'autonomists' in the history of science. Here also some authors stress the role of external factors and 'reduce' the progress of

---

[1] These final pages are based on an address given at Maastricht in July 1999 at the Graduation Ceremony of the students in the Magister Iuris Communis Programme.

science to the demands of trade, industry and warfare: for them modern science satisfied the requirements of modern capitalism and national defence. Other scholars, however, stress the 'autonomy' of the great inventors who, through successive centuries, searched for the laws of nature, following in the footsteps of their predecessors and discovering – or stumbling upon – the secrets of the material world and of the movement of the stars; they often pursued their seemingly irrelevant work in libraries and laboratories, irrespective of what society at large believed or wanted, and sometimes suffered for their discoveries at the hands of displeased dignitaries.

What concerns us more directly here is the road Europe is likely to take. Will the shaping of a European law – and the scholarly reflection on it – be determined by external pressure or will the internal strength of the system prevail and allow it to find its own way, adhering to its own intrinsic values? The outcome will, of course, depend on who 'the makers of the law' will be in twenty-first-century Europe – the courts, the Law Faculties or the elected assemblies. The answer to that crucial question is difficult to forecast, not only because it involves a good deal of crystal-ball gazing, which is not the historian's province, but also because different nations have traditionally approached this issue in different ways. Indeed, the age-old English instinct is to say, with Lord Denning, 'trust the judges, for they are the true guardians of the law'. The German feeling, which also goes back several centuries, is to say, with Savigny, 'trust the learned jurists, for they are the best guides through the thickets of the law'. The French instinct, on the other hand, is to say, in true Jacobin and Napoleonic vein, 'trust the legislator and beware of judges and jurists who pervert the codes'. As none of these traditions is the sole road to salvation, a truly European law ought to contain the most helpful elements of each one of them. This entails that legislators issue binding laws, that judges build a solid case law on those foundations, and that jurists provide the conceptual framework and the necessary reflection on the finality of the system as a whole. This may seem a daunting task, but it does not imply the creation of a body of law *ex nihilo*, since it will profit from the experience of many centuries in several countries. History has shown the usefulness of binding laws and codes for the certainty of the law, but also the merits of judicial creativity, as well as the advantages of a legal science which provides the required critical and fundamental reflection. Readers who shake their heads in disbelief might consider that the European Union has come about under their own unbelieving eyes. So why could the combined efforts of the Assemblies, the Faculties and the Bench not lead to a European law, that could emulate the Old European Age?

Legal history does not simply deal with a past that is over and done with: it deals with the past of Europe's future. It studies the antecedents of the challenges facing the lawyers who are entering the twenty-first century, one of which concerns European unification and more particularly the clash between internationalism and nativism. We cannot understand our predicament at the beginning of a new millennium unless we know and understand what brought us here. Two problems connected with European unification will no doubt engage the attention of the young lawyers of today, who are the leading jurists, judges, barristers and lawgivers of tomorrow: the unification of private law and the elaboration of a federal constitution.

In private law both universalism and localism have a powerful hold on the European mind. Both can boast of a great past, and neither will ever evict the other completely. Today's young lawyers naturally have the ambition to bring about change and to do better than their predecessors. They are too wise, however, to think they can change everything, emulating Cambacérès's illusion expressed in 1793 'de tout changer à la fois dans les écoles, dans les moeurs, dans les coutumes, dans les esprits, dans les lois d'un grand peuple'. They know that a legal system is like a large ocean-going vessel: one cannot suddenly bring it to a halt or change its course. These manoeuvres take time, as too brusque a movement might make the ship capsize or send her on the rocks. Nevertheless, change is necessary and change there will be.

European law in the twenty-first century will present a different face, in contract, intellectual property and civil procedure, and more generally in the whole area of private law. The rise of a common European jurisprudence – a new *ius commune* – is on the cards. It is, however, unlikely that this common doctrine will produce one civil code regulating every aspect for every country from Ireland to Poland (let alone the Urals). National and regional traditions and feelings are a reality we have to take into account, even though their importance should not be exaggerated, as some successful 'legal transplants' have shown. Nevertheless, as universalism and nativism are bound to clash, let us have a closer look at these two attitudes.

Universalism – one might also call it cosmopolitanism – is the ambition of jurists to create a law and a legal science that are valid for vast areas, surpassing local variation and even reaching a timeless validity based on pure reason. This global jurisprudence is separated from the culture which produced it and has its being outside history; it is the 'common law' of the scholars – if not of ordinary folk – and has no links with a particular country or ethnic or religious group.

Such was, as we have seen, the *ius commune* of the Old European Age, the lodestar of the small but influential cosmopolitan club of Latin-speaking jurists who studied and taught Roman and canon law from Aberdeen and Oxford to Cracow and Naples. Such also was its successor, the natural law of Grotius, Pufendorf and Domat, author of *Les Lois civiles dans leur ordre naturel* (the very title of whose work assumes that there is one natural order, and not one valid this side of the Pyrenees and another beyond them). This ambition to create universal norms deserves our admiration, for it is a noble aim and of respectable antiquity. Nevertheless, neither the *ius commune*, based on Justinian, nor the *ius naturale*, based on nature as perceived by reason, ever became the positive law of the European nation states and their codes: nativism and indigenous customs were too powerful. So, what is nativism – which one might also call nationalism, localism, regionalism or even parochialism (which it certainly was in the eyes of the enlightened judges and university-trained functionaries in the supreme courts and governments of modern Europe)? It describes the proud attachment of large kingdoms or small village communities to their national codes or customary laws. It stems from human diversity, a different past and a different environment. This *ius proprium* relates to people's own ways of doing things and expresses their national identities. Nativism rejects the notion that laws can and should be universalized, and feels, on the contrary, that they have grown naturally and organically in particular places and over particular periods of time.[2] Europeans will not turn into one grey mass of identical individuals who see the same films and watch the match between Manchester and Munich in their millions. Englishmen will be English and Germans will be German, and they will rejoice or weep accordingly. Localism means gut reactions and the simple cares of every day and everyman.

If law is part of the national character and if it is the expression of the *Volksgeist*, does a supranational European law stand a chance? There are, as we mentioned before, numerous 'legal transplants' to show that there is no need for despair. Justinian's *Corpus iuris* is probably the best illustration of a legal system crossing the most improbable cultural frontiers. This great encyclopaedia of ancient Roman wisdom was compiled and published as law, not in Rome but in Constantinople, in the Greek and not the Latin part of the empire where most Roman law had originated. This is where the first transplant of Roman law took place. The promulgation of this Latin lawbook for a Greek-speaking commonwealth led, of course, to problems of translation and interpretation. People in the sixth century tried to cope with them, but thereafter hardly anyone in the Byzantine empire learned Latin, nor were there any law schools. Consequently seventh- and eighth-century Byzantium was almost as ignorant of classical law as the Germanic kingdoms in the West. It was the merit of the emperors Basil the Macedonian (867–86) and

---

[2] See the reflections in I. Buruma, *Voltaire's coconuts* (London, 1999).

Leo VI the Wise (886–911) that they reversed this situation and, in the late ninth century, launched an ambitious programme for the rediscovery of the 'forgotten' lawbook of Justinian. Their main aspiration was to establish a reliable and complete Greek text of the *Corpus*, cleaned of old imperfections. Their endeavour was called the 'purification of the old laws' and amounted to what may be called the first Reception of Roman law, comparable to the one which took place in the West three hundred years later. On an elementary level the jurists compiled bilingual glossaries – conserved in more than a hundred manuscripts – and, on a more advanced level, devoted elaborate works to a more profound understanding and assimilation of classical legal thought. One famous result was the *Basilica* promulgated by Leo the Wise, a systematic re-codification in Greek of Justinian's lawbook, which led in its turn in the tenth century to glosses and commentaries. It should be noted that this Byzantine 'reception' was not considered a taking over of a foreign body: the East Roman empire saw itself as the continuation of ancient Rome, and its emperor styled himself 'basileus of the Romans'. Hence living according to ancient Roman law was no problem: 'Roman' and 'Byzantine' law were not different.[3]

In the West, the rediscovery of Justinian produced the *ius commune*, which became in its turn the *gemeines Recht*, the national law of modern Germany. Its latest flowering was the Pandectist School whose teaching passed into the *Bürgerliches Gesetzbuch*. And to cap it all, this Roman-German law was, in 1898, adopted as the Civil Code of westernized Japan. What happened to the poor *Volksgeist*, in this 'journey round the world in fifteen centuries' (and involving four languages, Latin, Greek, German and Japanese)?

The answer to the problem of universalism versus nationalism seems to be twofold. Firstly, let intrinsic quality rather than national sentiment be our guiding star. If localism corresponds to

---

3 We follow here the stimulating inaugural lecture by Professor M. T. Fögen, published under the title 'Brüssel, Beirut und Byzanz. Viele sprachen, ein Recht?', *Rechtshistorisches Journal* 12 (1993), 358–63.

sincerely held values in a given community, it should, of course, be granted due attention, but not if it is merely the dead wood of obsolete usages, whose *raison d'être* is lost in the mist of time. Secondly, the authorities should proceed with caution, not imposing a *Diktat* but seeking a consensus. Let us, if we introduce new codes, leave possibilities for escape routes in order not to hurt susceptibilities. We should, in other words, seek the *via media* between academic rootless cosmopolitanism and down-to-earth nativism. The defenders of both these attitudes should learn to understand each other's point of view and realize that both are legitimate and useful in their different ways. Europe has experienced this sort of peaceful co-existence in the past. Even the medieval Church, which was the ultimate model of universalism, knew local synodal legislation and tolerated a variety of customs in the margin of the great shared principles.[4] Nor does our own world ignore this sort of symbiosis: the examples of Scotland, southern Africa and Spain come readily to mind.[5]

If private law will occupy the minds of European lawyers, public law will demand no less attention: the European constitution will be the second challenge in the new century. A unified Europe that obliterates old nation states and turns itself into one vast centralized superpower, where national identities are drowned in a faceless bureaucracy, is neither possible nor desirable. But a loose alliance or mere customs union of the old sovereign states that

[4] See the remarks in C. R. Cheney, 'Legislation of the medieval English Church', *English Historical Review* 50 (1935), 193–224, 385–417 (repr. in C. R. Cheney, *The English Church and its laws, 12th–14th centuries,* I (London, 1982, Variorum Reprints).

[5] H. L. MacQueen, *Scots law and the road to the* Ius Commune (Maastricht, 2000, Ius Commune Lectures on European Private Law, 1); G. J. Van Niekerk, 'A common law for southern Africa: Roman law or indigenous African law?', in J. E. Spruit, W. J. Kamba and M. O. Minz (eds.), *Roman law at the crossroads* (Capetown, 2000), 83–102. See also the extensive chapter 4 devoted to the interaction of Roman-Dutch and English law in southern Africa in J. M. Smits, *Europees privaatrecht in wording. Naar een ius commune europaeum als gemengd rechtsstelsel* (Antwerp, Groningen, Oxford, 1999), 117–88. Studies on modern Spanish law have shown how much room was left for the native tradition of *fueros* and customs after the introduction of the Código Civil of 1889: B. Clavero, 'Nativism and transnationalism: Spanish law after the civil code', *Juristische Theoriebildung und rechtliche Einheit. Beiträge zu einem rechtshistorischen Seminar in Stockholm im September 1992* (Lund, 1993, Rättshistoriska Studier, 19), 25–35.

were responsible for terrible fratricidal warfare will not satisfy the dream of European unification which took shape at last after the Second World War. The obvious solution for this conundrum is a federal constitution, where existing countries and regions continue to function in direct contact with the people and their needs, but matters of common interest – defence, foreign policy, currency, protection of human rights – belong to a higher, federal authority. The contest between what the French call the *souverainistes* and the *fédéralistes* is still going on, but once a political decision is reached and the federal idea wins the day – as now seems likely – jurists will have to work out the appropriate legal system with all its nuts and bolts. One problem they will face concerns the different familiarity with the very notion of a federal constitution within Europe: German lawyers live in a federal republic and are naturally aware of the way it functions, but French lawyers, born and bred in the ideology of the *république une et indivisible*, have had no experience with federalism and, except for a few *comparatistes*, have never even heard of it. Such differences are an obvious stumbling block on the road to a European federal constitution and, as they have grown historically, it is appropriate here to have a look at the past.

For many centuries large political units were built by imperialist wars and forced assimilation. The Roman empire was the most impressive success story of Antiquity and a model for the unitary centralized Roman Church and the European nation states. The kingdoms of France and Spain are the outstanding examples of unitary monarchies built on the debris of regional fiefdoms; German history took the opposite road and ended up with a loose conglomerate of free territories and cities which were sometimes at war with each other and whose only imperial element was its name. While these opposite evolutions were going on, an interesting development took place in the Low Countries, where first under Burgundian and later Habsburg rule a nation state arose with a distinct constitution. The Seventeen Provinces of Emperor Charles V were less than a unitary monarchy but more than a loose alliance under a nominal head of state. They can best be described as a federal monarchy (as they consisted of seventeen dukedoms and counties, which all had their own political identity, courts, estates, privileges and customs). They had a common ruler and there were similar rules of succession ensuring that they would always remain together. Their union was, however, not merely personal, because they lived under common central – we could call them federal – governmental, fiscal and judicial councils. They were independent both of the kingdom of France and of the German empire so that they formed a new sovereign nation state which was perceived as such by the rest of Europe. After the revolt against Philip II and the rise of the Republic of the United Netherlands in the north, the existing structure was continued there: the Republic was a federation of seven sovereign provinces, but enjoyed common central institutions and acted on the European scene as one independent country. This federal experiment was a breakthrough in the history of constitutional law, as it was unknown to Roman imperial thinking. It acquired world-wide importance when it was adopted by the Thirteen Colonies in America, whose federal constitution was followed by several modern countries, most notably the Weimar Republic and the German Federal Republic. It is ironic that the country where it all started, the present-day kingdom of the Netherlands, gave up federalism in the early nineteenth century and became a unitary nation state.

Nowadays the federal formula, ensuring unity without oppression and offering a middle course between a crushing Jacobin unitarism and an anarchic array of local fiefdoms, is making headway. Interestingly this happens both at the European level – with a European government, law courts and parliament – and in some old nation states: the regionalization in Italy and Spain and the federalization of Belgium come to mind, but the most exciting experiment is taking place at this very moment in the United Kingdom, where the identity of Scotland and to a lesser degree Wales and Northern Ireland is recognized and expressed in distinct governmental organs. This may one day even lead to a separate English assembly and an overriding

British parliament for the four parts of the United Kingdom. The novelty of this development, which is alien to British constitutional traditions, predictably upsets some observers, who grumble about a disunited United Kingdom. Others, however, see it as a positive development which, far from breaking up the present kingdom, will safeguard it by achieving a necessary adaptation to new popular moods and needs. Whatever the future holds, federalism, which recognizes regional aspirations and cultural minorities instead of alienating them, will need the skills of our jurists, both at the national and the European level. It is an interesting thought that while Britain is taking the federal road within its borders, it still seems to be offended by the notion of a European federation. This is allegedly because of its attachment to absolute parliamentary sovereignty which in reality, because of the supranational authority of European treaties, legislation and judicial decisions which override the national law of all member states, already belongs to the past.[6]

---

[6] See the reflections in H. Young's recent work *This blessed plot: Britain and Europe from Churchill to Blair* (London, 1999).

Bibliography

This bibliography is not a list of all works quoted in this book, but an orientation for further reading.

INTERNATIONAL

Allen, C. K., *Law in the making*, 7th edn, Oxford, 1964

Anners, E., *Den Europeiske rettens historie*, 4th edn, Oslo, 1991

Ascheri, M., *Diritto medievale e moderno. Problemi del processo, della cultura e delle fonti giuridiche*, Rimini, 1991

Baker, J. H. (ed.), *Judicial records, law reports, and the growth of case law*, Berlin, 1989; Comparative Studies in Continental and Anglo-American Legal History, 5

Bellomo, M., *L'Europa del diritto comune*, 6th edn, Rome, 1993

Bergh, G. C. J. J. van den, *Geleerd recht. Een geschiedenis van de Europese rechtswetenschap in vogelvlucht*, 2nd edn, Deventer, 1985

Berman, H. J., *Law and revolution. The formation of the western legal tradition*, Cambridge, Mass., 1983

Bieresborn, D., *Klage und Klageerwiderung im deutschen und englischen Zivilprozess. Eine rechtshistorische und rechtsvergleichende Untersuchung unter besonderer Berücksichtigung der Beeinflussung durch das römisch-kanonische Verfahren*, Frankfurt, 1999; Rechtshistorische Reihe, 195

Bossy, J., *Disputes and settlements. Law and human relations in the West*, Cambridge, 1983

Büchler, T., *Rechtsquellenlehre*, I: *Gewohnheitsrecht, Enquête, Kodifikation*, II: *Rechtsquellentypen, Rechtserzeugung, Rechtserfragung, Legitimität der Rechtsquellen*, Zürich, 1977–85; 3 vols.

Caenegem, R. C. van, *Legal history: A European perspective*, London and Rio Grande, 1991 [Collection of articles]

    An historical introduction to private law, Cambridge, 1992 (rep. 1994)

    Judges, legislators and professors. Chapters in European legal history, 2nd edn, Cambridge, 1993

International 145

Law, history, the Low Countries and Europe, ed. by L. Milis *et al.*, London and Rio Grande, 1994 [Collection of articles]

Calasso, F., *Medio evo del diritto*, I: *Le fonti*, Milan, 1954

Caravale, M., *Ordinamenti giuridici dell'Europa medievale*, Bologna, 1994

Carbasse, J. M. and Depambour-Tarride, L. (eds.), *La conscience du juge dans la tradition juridique européenne*, Paris, 1998

Caroni, P., *Privatrecht. Eine sozialhistorische Einführung*, Basle and Frankfurt, 1988

Cavanna, A., *Storia del diritto moderno in Europa. Le fonti ed il pensiero giuridico*, Milan, 2nd edn, 1982

Coing, H., *Europäisches Privatrecht 1500 bis 1800*, I: *Älteres Gemeines Recht*, II: *19. Jahrhundert. Überblick über die Entwicklung des Privatrechts in den ehemals gemeinrechtlichen Ländern*, Munich, 1985–89; 2 vols.

Coing, H. (ed.), *Handbuch der Quellen und Literatur der neueren europäischen Privatrechtsgeschichte*, I: *Mittelalter (1100–1500). Die gelehrten Rechte und die Gesetzgebung*, Munich, 1973; II: *Neuere Zeit (1500–1800). Das Zeitalter des gemeinen Rechts*, 1. Teilband: *Wissenschaft*, 1972; 2. Teilband: *Gesetzgebung und Rechtsprechung*, 1976; III: *Das 19. Jahrhundert*, 1. Teilband: *Gesetzgebung zum allgemeinen Privatrecht*, 1982; 2. Teilband: *Gesetzgebung zum allgemeinen Privatrecht und zum Verfahrensrecht*, 1982; 3. Teilband: *Gesetzgebung zu den privatrechtlichen Sondergebieten*, 1986; 4. Teilband: *Die nordischen Länder*, 1987; 5. Teilband: *Südosteuropa*, 1988

Cortese, E., *La norma giuridica. Spunti teorici nel diritto comune classico*, Milan, 1962–4; 2 vols.

Il rinascimento giuridico medievale, Rome, 1992.

Il diritto nella storia medievale, I: *L'alto medioevo*, II: *Il basso medioevo*, Rome, 1995; 2 vols.

David, R., *Les grands systèmes de droit contemporains*, 3rd edn, Paris, 1969; Précis Dalloz

Davies, W. and Fouracre, P. (eds.), *The settlement of disputes in early medieval Europe*, Cambridge, 1986

Dekkers, R., *Le droit privé des peuples. Caractères, destinées, dominantes*, Brussels, 1953

Denzer, H., *Moralphilosophie und Naturrecht bei Samuel Pufendorf. Eine geistes- und wissenschaftsgeschichtliche Untersuchung zur Geburt des Naturrechts aus der praktischen Philosophie*, Munich, 1972

d'Entrèves, A. P., *Natural law. An historical survey*, 2nd edn, London, 1970

Feenstra, R. en Ahsmann, M., *Contract. Aspecten van de begrippen contract en contractvrijheid in historisch perspectief*, 2nd edn, Deventer, 1988; Rechtshistorische Cahiers, 2

Gagnér, S., *Studien zur Ideengeschichte der Gesetzgebung*, Stockholm, 1960; Acta Universitatis Upsaliensis. Studia Iuridica Upsaliensia, 1

Gans, E., *Naturrecht und Universalrechtsgeschichte*, ed. and intr. by M. Riedel, Stuttgart, 1981; Deutscher Idealismus, 2

Ganshof, F. L., *Recherches sur les capitulaires*, Paris, 1958; Société d'Histoire du Droit
Qu'est-ce que la féodalité?, 5th edn, Paris, 1982

Gaudemet, J., *Les Naissances du droit. Le Temps, le pouvoir et la science au service du droit*, Paris, 1997

Gilissen, J., *Introduction au droit. Esquisse d'une histoire universelle du droit. Les sources du droit depuis le XIIIe siècle. Eléments d'une histoire du droit privé*, Brussels, 1979

Gilmore, B., *The death of contract*, Columbus, Ohio, 1974

Gordley, J. R., *The philosophical origins of modern contract doctrine*, Oxford, 1991

Goyard-Fabre, S., *Pufendorf et le droit naturel*, Paris, 1994

Grossi, P., *L'ordine giuridico medievale*, Rome and Bari, 1995

Guterman, S., *From personal to territorial law. Aspects of the history and structure of the Western legal-constitutional tradition*, Metuchen, N.J., 1972

Guzman, A., *Ratio scripta*, Frankfurt, 1981; Ius commune. Sonderhefte, Texte und Monographien, 14

Hallebeek, J., *The concept of unjust enrichment in late scholasticism*, Nijmegen, 1996

Halpérin, J.-L., *Entre nationalisme juridique et communauté de droit*, Paris, 1999

Hannig, J., *Consensus fidelium. Frühfeudale Interpretationen des Verhältnisses von Königtum und Adel am Beispiel des Frankenreichs*, Stuttgart, 1982; Monographien zur Geschichte des Mittelalters, 27

Hartkamp, A. S. *et al.* (eds.), *Towards a European civil code*, Nijmegen etc., 1994

Hattenhauer, H. and Buschmann, A., *Textbuch zur Privatrechtsgeschichte der Neuzeit mit Übersetzungen*, Munich, 1967

Hilaire, J., *Le droit des affaires et l'histoire*, Paris, 1995.

Ibbetson, D., *An historical introduction to the law of obligations*, Oxford, 1999

Jacob, R. (ed.), *Le juge et le jugement dans les traditions juridiques européennes. Etude d'histoire comparée*, Paris, 1996; Droit et Société, 17. [Papers of a Paris colloquium of 1993]

Jakobs, H. H., *Die Begründung der geschichtlichen Rechtswissenschaft*, Paderborn, 1992; Rechts- und Staatswissenschaftliche Veröffentlichungen der Görres-Gesellschaft, N.F. 63

Kaufmann, E., *Aequitatis iudicium. Königsgericht und Billigkeit in der Rechtsordnung des frühen Mittelalters*, Frankfurt, 1959

Kelley, D. R., *The human measure. Social thought in the Western legal tradition*, Cambridge, Mass., 1990

Kelly, J. M., *A short history of western legal theory*, Oxford, 1992

King, P. D., *Law and society in the Visigothic kingdom*, Cambridge, 1972; Cambridge Studies in Medieval Life and Thought

Kleinheyer, G. and Schröder, J. (eds.), *Deutsche und europäische Juristen aus neun Jahrhunderten. Eine biographische Einführung in die Geschichte der Rechtswissenschaft*, 4th edn, Heidelberg, 1996.

Koschaker, P., *Europa und das römische Recht*, Munich and Berlin, 1947

Kroeschell, K. and Cordes, A. (eds.), *Funktion und Form. Quellen und Methodenprobleme der mittelalterlichen Rechtsgeschichte*, Berlin, 1996; Schriften zur Europäischen Rechts- und Verfassungsgeschichte, 8

Lawson, F. H., *A common lawyer looks at the civil law*, Ann Arbor, 1955; The Thomas M. Cooley Lectures, Fifth Series

Lieberwirth, R., *Christian Thomasius. Sein wissenschaftliches Lebenswerk*, Weimar, 1955

Lokin, J. H. A. and Zwalve, W. J., *Inleiding tot de rechtsgeschiedenis*, Groningen, 1985

Hoofdstukken uit de Europese Codificatiegeschiedenis, Groningen, 1986

Lupoi, M., *Alle radici del mondo giuridico europeo. Saggio storico-comparativo*, Rome, 1994; Engl. transl.: *On the origins of the European legal order*, Cambridge, 1999

McKitterick, R., *The Carolingians and the written word*, Cambridge, 1989

MacQueen, H. L., *Scots law and the road to the ius commune*, Maastricht, 2000; Ius Commune Lectures on European Private Law, 1

Markesinis, B. S. (ed.), *The gradual convergence. Foreign ideas, foreign influences and English law on the eve of the twenty-first century*, Oxford, 1994

Mehren, A. T. von and Gordley, J. R., *The civil law system: An introduction to the comparative study of law*, 2nd edn, Boston, Toronto, 1977 [Contains an extensive historical introduction]

Mellinkoff, D., *The language of the law*, Boston, Toronto, 1963

Merryman, J. H., *The civil law tradition. An introduction to the legal systems of Western Europe and Latin America*, Stanford, 1969

Moccia, L. (ed.), *I giudici di pace. Storia, comparazione, riforma*, Milan, 1996 [Papers of Colloquium in Macerata in 1995]

Mohnhaupt, H. (ed.), *Zur Geschichte des Familien- und Erbrechts. Untersuchungen und Perspektiven*, Frankfurt, 1987; Ius Commune, Sonderhefte, 32

Mohnhaupt, H. and Simon, D. (eds.), *Vorträge zur Justizforschung. Geschichte und Theorie*, I, Frankfurt am Main, 1992; Rechtsprechung. Materialien und Studien, Veröffentlichungen des Max-Planck-Instituts für Europäische Rechtsgeschichte, 4

Nanz, K. P., *Die Entstehung des allgemeinen Vertragsbegriffs im 16 und 18 Jahrhundert*, Munich, 1985; Beiträge zur Neueren Privatrechtsgeschichte, 9

Neusüss, W., *Gesunde Vernunft und Natur der Sache. Studien zur juristischen Argumentation im 18. Jahrhundert*, Berlin, 1970

Padoa-Schioppa, A., *Saggi di storia del diritto commerciale*, Milan, 1992

Pauw, F. de, *Grotius and the law of the sea*, Brussels, 1965

Pound, R., *Interpretations of legal history*, Cambridge, Mass., 1946

Prest, W. (ed.), *Lawyers in early modern Europe and America*, London, 1981

Ridderikhoff, C. M., *Jean Pyrrhus d'Anglebermes. Rechtswetenschap en humanisme aan de Universiteit van Orleans in het begin van de 16de eeuw*, Leiden, 1981

Robinson, O. F., Fergus, T. D. and Gordon, W. M., *An introduction to European legal history*, Abingdon, 1985

Samuel von Pufendorf 1632–1982. Ett rättshistorisk symposium i Lund 15–20 Jan., 1982, Stockholm, 1986; Skrifter Utgivna av Institutet för Rättshistorisk Forskning, serien II; Rättshistoriska Studier, 12

Schlosser, H., Sturm, F. and Weber, H., *Die rechtsgeschichtliche Exegese. Römisches Recht, Deutsches Recht, Kirchenrecht*, 2nd edn, Munich, 1993

Schrage, E. J. H., *Non quia romanum sed quia ius. Das Entstehen eines europäischen Rechtsbewusstseins im Mittelalter*, Goldbach, 1996; Bibliotheca Eruditorum, 17

Schrage, E. J. H. (ed.), *Unjust enrichment. The comparative legal history of the law of restitution*, Berlin, 1995; Comparative Studies in Continental and Anglo-American Legal History, 15

Schulze, R. (ed.), *Europäische Rechts- und Verfassungsgeschichte. Ergebnisse und Perspektiven der Forschung*, Berlin, 1991; Schriften zur Europäischen Rechts- und Verfassungsgeschichte, 3

Seagle, W., *The quest for law*, New York, 1941 (= *Weltgeschichte des Rechts. Einführung in die Probleme und Erscheinungsformen des Rechts*, 3rd edn, Munich and Berlin, 1967)

Sellert, W. (ed.), *Das Gesetz in Spätantike und früherem Mittelalter*, Göttingen, 1992

International   149

Smits, J., *Europees privaatrecht in wording. Naar een Ius Commune Europaeum als gemengd rechtsstelsel*, Antwerp, Groningen, Oxford, 1999

Spruit, J. E. *et al.* (eds.), *Roman law at the crossroads*, Capetown, 2000

Stein, P., *Legal institutions. The development of dispute settlement*, London, 1984

Roman law in European history, Cambridge, 1999

Strömholm, S., *A short history of legal thinking in the West*, Stockholm, 1985

Tarello, G., *Le ideologie della codificazione nel secolo XVIII*, I, Genoa, 1971

Thieme, H., *Naturrecht und europäische Privatrechtsgeschichte*, 2nd edn, Basle, 1954

Vanderlinden, J., *Le concept de code en Europe occidentale du XIIIe au XIXe siècle. Essai de définition*, Brussels, 1967

Watson, A., *The making of the civil law*, Cambridge, Mass., 1981

The Evolution of law, Baltimore, 1985 [Continuation in: 'The Evolution of law: Continued', *Law and History Review*, 5, 1987, 537–70]

Legal transplants. An approach to comparative law, 2nd edn, Athens, Ga., London, 1993

Sources of law. Legal change and ambiguity, 2nd edn, Philadelphia, 1998

Welzer, H., *Die Naturrechtslehre Samuel Pufendorfs*, Berlin, 1958

Wenskus, R., *Stammesbildung und Verfassung. Das Werden der frühmittelalterlichen Gentes*, Cologne, Graz, 1961

Wieacker, F., *Privatrechtsgeschichte der Neuzeit unter besonderer Berücksichtigung der deutschen Entwicklung*, 2nd edn, Göttingen, 1967. Eng. tr. by T. Weir, *A history of private law in Europe, with particular reference to Germany*, Oxford, 1995

Wijffels, A. (ed.), *Case law in the making? The techniques and methods of judicial records and law reports*, Berlin, 1997; 2 vols.; Comparative Studies in Continental and Anglo-American Legal History, 17, 1, 2

Wolf, A., *Gesetzgebung in Europa 1100–1500. Zur Entstehung der Territorialstaaten*, 2nd edn, Munich, 1996 [Based on Wolf's chapter in Coing's *Handbuch*, I]

Wolf, E., *Das Problem der Naturrechtslehre. Versuch einer Orientierung*, 2nd edn, Karlsruhe, 1964

World of Hugo Grotius (1583–1645). The Proceedings of the International Colloquium Organized by the Grotius Committee of the Royal Netherlands Academy of Arts and Sciences 1983; Amsterdam and Maarssen, 1984

Zane, J. M., *The story of law*, 2nd edn, Indianapolis, 1999

Zimmermann, R., *The law of obligations. Roman foundations of the civilian tradition*, Capetown, Munich, 1990

Zimmermann, R. (ed.), *Amerikanische Rechtskultur und europäisches Privat-
recht. Impressionen aus der Neuen Welt*, Tübingen, 1995
Zweigert, K. and Kötz, H., *Einführung in die Rechtsvergleichung auf dem
Gebiete des Privatrechts*, 2nd edn, Tübingen, 1984; 2 vols.; Eng. tr.:
An introduction to comparative law, by T. Weir, Amsterdam, 1977; 2
vols. [Vol. 1 contains much historical material]

ROMAN AND CANON LAW

Bellomo, M., *Saggio sull'università nell'età del diritto comune*, Catania, 1979
Brundage, J. A., *Medieval canon law*, London, New York, 1995
Dahyot-Dolivet, H., *Précis d'histoire du droit canonique. Fondement et évolution*,
Rome, 1984; Utrumque Jus, 10
Diurni, G., *L'expositio ad Librum Papiensem e la scienza giuridica preirner-
iana*, Rome, 1976; Biblioteca della Rivista di Storia del Diritto
Italiano, 23
Errera, A., *Arbor Actionum. Genere letterario e forma di classificazione delle
azioni nella dottrina dei glossatori*, Bologna, 1995
Feenstra, R., *Fata Iuris Romani. Etudes d'histoire du droit*, Leiden, 1974
Feine, H. E., *Kirchliche Rechtsgeschichte. Die Katholische Kirche*, 5th edn,
Cologne, Graz, 1972
Fowler-Magerl, L., *Ordo iudiciorum vel ordo iudiciarius. Begriff und Literatur-
gattung*, Frankfurt, 1984; Ius Commune. Sonderhefte, 19
Gaudemet, J., *Les Sources du droit canonique VIIIe–XXe siècle. Repères cano-
niques. Sources occidentales*, Paris, 1993; Collection Droit Canonique.
Etudes
Eglise et cité. Histoire du droit canonique, Paris, 1994
Gilmore, M. P., *Humanists and jurists*, Cambridge, Mass., 1963
Helmholz, R., *The spirit of classical canon law*, Athens, Ga., 1996
Hove, A. van, *Prolegomena*, 2nd edn, Mechelen, Rome, 1945; Commen-
tarium Lovaniense in Codicem Iuris Canonici, I, 1
Ius romanum medii aevi, ed. E. Genzmer, Milan, 1961 ff.
Jakobs, H. H., *De similibus ad similia bei Bracton und Azo*, Frankfurt, 1996;
Ius Commune. Sonderhefte, 87
Kisch, G., *Erasmus und die Jurisprudenz seiner Zeit. Studien zum humanistischen
Rechtsdenken*, Basle, 1960
Lange, H., *Römisches Recht im Mittelalter*, I: *Die Glossatoren*, Munich, 1997
Le Bras, G., *Institutions ecclésiastiques de la Chrétienté médiévale*, Paris, 1959–
64; 2 vols.; *Histoire de l'église*, ed. by A. Fliche and V. Martin, XII,
1, 2

Le Bras, G. (ed.), *Histoire des institutions et du droit de l'église en occident*, Paris, 1955 ff.

Legendre, P., *La pénétration du droit romain dans le droit canonique classique de Gratien à Innocent IV*, Paris, 1964

Levy, E., *West Roman vulgar law: The law of property*, Philadelphia, 1961; Memoirs of the American Philosophical Society, 29

Lewis, A. D. E. and Ibbetson, D. J. (eds.), *The Roman law tradition*, Cambridge, 1994

McIntyre, J. P., *Customary law in the Corpus Iuris Canonici*, San Francisco, 1990

Maffei, D., *Gli inizi dell'umanesimo giuridico*, Milan, 1956

Meijers, E. M., *Etudes d'histoire du droit*, ed. by R. Feenstra and H. F. W. D. Fischer, Leiden, 1956–73; 4 vols.

Owen, D. M., *The medieval canon law: Teaching, literature and transmission*, Cambridge, 1990

Plöchl, W., *Geschichte des Kirchenrechts*, Vienna, I, 2nd edn, 1960, II, 2nd edn, 1962, III, 1959, IV, 1966

Schrage, E. J. H. (ed.), *Das römische Recht im Mittelalter*, Darmstadt, 1987; Wege der Forschung, 635 [Reprints articles by Genzmer, Seckel, Kantorowicz, and an up-to-date bibliography on Roman law 1100–1500 by R. Feenstra]

Schrage, E. J. H., with Dondorp, H., *Utrumque Ius. Een inleiding tot de studie van de bronnen van het middeleeuwse geleerde recht*, Amsterdam, 1987

Smith, J. A. C., *Medieval law teachers and writers, civilian and canonist*, Ottawa, 1975

Speciale, G., *La memoria del diritto comune. Sulle tracce d'uso del Codex di Giustiniano (sec. XII–XV)*, Rome, 1995; Coll. I Libri di Erice, 10

Stein, P., *The character and influence of the Roman civil law. Historical essays*, London and Ronceverte, 1988

Troje, H. E., *Humanistische Jurisprudenz. Studien zur europäischen Rechtswissenschaft unter dem Einfluss des Humanismus*, Goldbach, 1993; Bibliotheca Eruditorum, 6

Ullmann, W., *The medieval idea of law as represented by Lucas de Penna. A study in fourteenth-century legal scholarship*, London, 1946

Waelkens, L., *La théorie de la coutume chez Jacques de Révigny. Edition et analyse de sa répétition sur la loi de quibus (D.1.3.32)*, Leiden, 1984

Weimar, P. (ed.), *Die Renaissance der Wissenschaften im 12. Jahrhundert*, Zurich, 1981; Zürcher Hochschulforum, 2

BELGIUM AND THE NETHERLANDS

Ahsmann, M., *Collegia en colleges. Juridisch onderwijs aan de Leidse Universiteit 1575–1630 in het bijzonder het disputeren*, Groningen, 1990; Rechtshistorische Studies, n.s. 1

Bergh, G. C. J. J. van den, *The life and work of Gerard Noodt (1647–1725). Dutch legal scholarship between humanism and enlightenment*, Oxford, 1988

Blécourt, A. S. de and Fischer, H. F. W. D., *Kort begrip van het oudvaderlands burgerlijk recht*, 7th edn, Groningen, 1967 [repr. of 7th edn of 1959, but with addendum by J. A. Ankum]

Brink, H. van den, *Rechtsgeschiedenis bij wijze van inleiding*, Deventer, 1976

Cerutti, F. F. X., *Hoofdstukken uit de Nederlandse rechtsgeschiedenis*, Nijmegen, 1972

Dekkers, R., *Bibliotheca Belgica Juridica. Een bio-bibliografisch overzicht der rechtsgeleerdheid in de Nederlanden van de vroegste tijden af tot 1800*, Brussels, 1951; Verhand. Kon. Vl. Acad. Wetensch., Kl. Lett., XIII, 14

Dievoet, E. van, *Het burgerlijk recht in België en in Nederland van 1800 tot 1940. De rechtsbronnen*, Antwerp and The Hague, 1943

Erauw, J. and Bouckaert, B. (eds.), *Liber memorialis François Laurent 1810–87*, Brussels, 1989

Feenstra, R., *Romeinsrechtelijke grondslagen van het Nederlands privaatrecht. Inleidende hoofdstukken*, 4th edn, Leiden, 1984

Gerbenzon, P. and Algra, N. E., *Voortgangh des rechtes*, 5th edn, Alphen aan den Rijn, 1979

Gilissen, J., *Historische inleiding tot het recht*, II: *De bronnen van het recht in de Belgische gewesten sedert de dertiende eeuw*, 2nd edn, by M. Magits, Antwerp, 1989

Godding, P., *Le droit privé dans les Pays-Bas méridionaux du 12e au 18e siècle*, 2nd edn, Brussels, 1991; Académie Royale de Belgique, Classe des Lettres

Le Conseil de Brabant sous le règne de Philippe le Bon (1430–1467), Brussels, 1998

Goede, A. de, *Nederlandse Rechtsgeschiedenis*, 2 vols., Leiden, Amsterdam, 1949–53

Heijden, E. J. J. van der, *Aantekeningen bij de geschiedenis van het oude vaderlandse recht*, 7th edn by B. H. D. Hermesdorf, Nijmegen, Utrecht, 1965

Heirbaut, D., *Over heren vazallen en graven. Het persoonlijk leenrecht in Vlaanderen ca. 1000–1305*, Brussels, 1997

Hermesdorf, B. H. D., *Rechtsspiegel. Een rechtshistorische terugblik in de Lage Landen van het Herfsttij*, ed. by P. J. Verdam, Nijmegen, 1980

Holthöfer, E., *Beiträge zur Justizgeschichte der Niederlande, Belgien und Luxemburg im 19. und 20. Jahrhundert*, Frankfurt, 1993

Jansen, G. J. H., *Natuurrecht of Romeins Recht. Een studie over leven en werk van F. A. van der Marck (1719–1800) in het licht van de opvattingen van zijn tijd*, Leiden, 1987

Kooiker, H., *Lex scripta abrogata: De derde Renaissance van het Romeinse recht. Een onderzoek naar de doorwerking van het oude recht na de invoering van civielrechtelijke codificaties in het begin van de negentiende eeuw*, I: *De uitwendige ontwikkeling*, Nijmegen, 1996, Doct. Diss.

Kop, P. C., *Legisme en privaatrechtswetenschap. Legisme in de Nederlandse privaatrechtswetenschap in de negentiende eeuw*, Deventer, 1982; Rechtshistorische Cahiers (ed. G. C. J. J. van den Bergh and R. Feenstra), 3

Kunst, A. J. M., *Korte voorgeschiedenis van het Nederlands Burgerlijk Wetboek*, Zwolle, 1967; Uitgaven van het Molengraaf Instituut voor Privaatrecht te Utrecht, 1

Historische Ontwikkeling van het Recht, I, 2nd edn, Zwolle, 1969, II, 1968

Maes, L. T., *Recht heeft vele significaties. Rechtshistorische opstellen*, Brussels, 1979

Martyn, G., *Het eeuwig edict van 12 juli 1611. Zijn genese en zijn rol in de verschriftelijking van het privaatrecht*, Brussels, 2000; Algemeen Rijksarchief en Rijksarchief in de Provinciën, Studia, 81

Monté Ver Loren, J. P. de, *Hoofdlijnen van de ontwikkeling der rechterlijke organisatie in de Noordelijke Nederlanden tot de Bataafse omwenteling*, 5th edn by J. E. Spruit, Deventer, 1972

Nève, P. and Coppens, C. (eds.), *Die rechtswissenschaftlichen Beziehungen zwischen den Niederlanden und Deutschland in historischer Sicht*, Nijmegen, 1991

Rhee, C. H. van, *Litigation and legislation. Civil procedure at first instance in the Great Council for the Netherlands in Malines (1522–1559)*, Brussels, 1997

Smidt, J. T. de et al., *Compendium van de Geschiedenis van het Nederlands Privaatrecht*, 3rd edn, Deventer, 1977; with R. Feenstra

Spanoghe, E. and Feenstra, R. (eds.), *Honderdvijftig jaar rechtsleven in België en Nederland 1830–1980*, Leiden, 1981; Leidse Juridische Reeks, XV

Strubbe, E. I., *De luister van ons oude recht. Verzamelde rechtshistorische studies,* Brussels, 1973; Rijksuniv. Gent, Publicaties van de Faculteit der Rechtsgeleerdheid, 5

Verdam, P. J., *Nederlandse rechtsgeschiedenis 1975–1795* [sic], Alphen aan den Rijn, 1976

Verhas, C. M. O., *De beginjaren van de Hoge Raad van Holland, Zeeland en West-Friesland,* The Hague, 1997

Warlomont, R., *François Laurent juriste, homme d'action et publiciste,* Brussels, 1948

Wijffels, A., *Les allégations du droit savant dans les dossiers du Grand Conseil de Malines (causes septentrionales, c. 1460–1580),* Leiden, 1985; 2 vols.; Rechtshistorische Studies, 11

Zeylemaker, H., *Geschiedenis van de wetenschap van het burgerlijk procesrecht (praktijkrecht) in Nederland van de aanvang tot 1913,* Amsterdam, 1952; Geschiedenis der Nederlandse Rechtswetenschap, IV, 1

ENGLAND

Abel-Smith, B. and Stevens, R., *Lawyers and the courts. A sociological study of the English legal system 1750–1965,* London, 1967

Anderson, J. S., *Lawyers and the making of English land law, 1832–1940,* Oxford, 1992

Atiyah, P. S., *The rise and fall of freedom of contract,* Oxford, 1979

Baker, J. H., *An introduction to English legal history,* 3rd edn, London, 1990

Baker, J. H. (ed.), *Judicial records, law reports and the growth of case law,* Berlin, 1989; Comparative Studies in Continental and Anglo-American Legal History, 5

Baker, J. H. and Milsom, S. F. C., *Sources of English legal history. Private law to 1750,* London, 1986

Bush, J. A. and Wijffels, A. (eds.), *Learning the law. Teaching and the transmission of law in England 1150–1900,* London and Rio Grande, 1999 [Papers of the XIIIth British Legal History Conference, Cambridge, 1997]

Caenegem, R. C. van, *The birth of the English common law,* 2nd edn, Cambridge, 1988

Cantor, N., *Imagining law. Common law and the foundations of the American legal system,* New York, 1997

Cornish, W. R. and Clark, G. de N., *Law and society in England 1750–1950,* London, 1989

Duman, D., *The judicial bench in England 1727–1875: The reshaping of a professional elite*, London, 1982; Royal Historical Society

Elton, G. R., *English law in the sixteenth century: Reform in an age of change*, London, 1979; Selden Society lecture

F. W. Maitland, London, 1985

Fifoot, C. H. S., *Judge and jurist in the reign of Victoria*, London, 1959

Fleming, R., *Domesday Book and the law. Society and legal custom in early medieval England*, Cambridge, 1998

Heward, E., *Lord Denning*, 2nd edn, Chichester, 1997

Hill, L. M., *Bench and bureaucracy. The public career of Sir Julius Caesar, 1580–1606*, Cambridge, 1988

Holdsworth, W. S., *History of English law*, London, 1903–72; 17 vols. [Several vols. have been re-edited; vols. XIV–XVI ed. posthumously by A. L. Goodhart and H. G. Hanbury; vol. XVII is a General Index by J. Burke]

Hudson, J., *Land, law and lordship in Anglo-Norman England*, Oxford, 1994

The formation of the English common law. Law and society in England from the Norman Conquest to Magna Carta, London, 1996

Hudson, J. (ed.), *The history of English law. Centenary essays on 'Pollock and Maitland'*, Oxford, 1996; Proceedings of the British Academy, 89

Kelly, P. J., *Utilitarianism and distributive justice: Jeremy Bentham and the civil law*, Oxford, 1990

Levack, B. P., *The civil lawyers in England 1603–41. A political study*, Oxford, 1973

Lobban, M., *The common law and English jurisprudence 1760–1850*, Oxford, 1991

Manchester, A. H., *A modern legal history of England and Wales 1750–1950*, London, 1980

Sources of English legal history. Law, history and society in England and Wales 1750–1950, London, 1984

Markesinis, B. S., *Foreign law and foreign ideas in the English courts*, Amsterdam, 1998; Koninklijke Nederlandse Akademie van Wetenschappen, Mededelingen Afd. Letterkunde, new series, 61, 7

Melikan, R., *John Scott, Lord Eldon 1751–1838*, Cambridge, 1999; Cambridge Studies in English Legal History

Milsom, S. F. C., *Historical foundations of the common law*, London, 1969

Oldham, J., *The Mansfield manuscripts and the growth of English law in the eighteenth century*, Chapel Hill, N.C., 1992; 2 vols.

Plucknett, T. F. T., *Legislation of Edward I*, Oxford, 1949
A concise history of the common law, 5th edn, London, 1956

Pollock F. and Maitland, F. W., *The history of English law before the time of Edward I*, 2nd edn, Cambridge, 1968; 2 vols.

Postema, G. J., *Bentham and the common law tradition*, Oxford, 1986

Prichard, M. J. and Yale, D. E. C. (eds.), *Hale and Fleetwood on Admiralty jurisdiction*, London, 1993; Selden Soc. Publ., 108

Richardson, H. G. and Sayles, G. O., *The governance of mediaeval England from the Conquest to Magna Carta*, Edinburgh, 1963
Law and legislation from Aethelberht to Magna Carta, Edinburgh, 1966

Rubin, R. R. and Sugarman, D. (eds.), *Law, economy and society. Essays in the history of English law 1750–1914*, Abingdon, 1984

Rumble, W. E., *The thought of John Austin: Jurisprudence, colonial reform and the British constitution*, London, 1985

Simpson, A. W. B., *A history of the common law of contract. The rise of the action of assumpsit*, Oxford, 1975
Leading cases in the common law, Oxford, 1995
Victorian law and the industrial spirit, London, 1995; Selden Society Lecture

Stevens, R., *Law and politics. The House of Lords as a judicial body, 1800–1976*, London, 1979

Stewart, R., *H. B.: The public career of Henry Brougham 1778–1868*, London, 1985

Teeven, K. M., *A history of the Anglo-American common law of contract*, New York, London, 1990

Wormald, P., *The making of English law. King Alfred to the twelfth century*, I: *Legislation and its limits*, Oxford, 1999

Yale, D. E. C. (ed.), *Lord Nottingham's Chancery Cases*, London, 1961; Selden Soc. Publ., 79

FRANCE

Arnaud, A.-J., *Les origines doctrinales du Code civil français*, Paris, 1969
Essai d'analyse structurale du Code civil français. La Règle du jeu dans la paix bourgeoise, Paris, 1973; Bibliothèque de Philosophie du Droit
Les juristes face à la société du XIXe siècle à nos jours, Paris, 1975; Coll. SUP. Le Juriste (dir. J. Carbonnier), 7

Aubenas, R., *Cours d'histoire du droit privé. Anciens pays de droit écrit*, I, Aix en Provence, 1956

Bart, J., *Histoire du droit privé, de la chute de l'Empire romain au XIXe siècle*, Paris, 1998

Bouckaert, B., *De exegetische school. Een kritische studie van de rechtsbronnen-en interpretatieleer bij de 19de eeuwse commentatoren van de Code civil*, Antwerp, 1981

Bredin, J.-D., *Sieyès: La Clé de la Révolution française*, Paris, 1988

Brown, E. A. R. and Famiglietti, R. C., *The 'Lit de Justice': Semantics, ceremonial, and the Parlement of Paris. 1300–1600*, Sigmaringen, 1994; Beihefte der Francia, 31

Bürge, A., *Das französische Privatrecht im 19. Jahrhundert. Zwischen Tradition und Pandektenwissenschaft. Liberalismus und Etatismus*, Frankfurt, 1991; Ius Commune. Sonderhefte, 52

Carbasse, J.-M., *Introduction historique au droit*, Paris, 1998

Chêne, C., *L'Enseignement du droit français en pays de droit écrit (1679–1793)*, Geneva, 1982; Travaux d'Histoire Ethico-politique, XXXIX

Craveri, P., *Ricerche sulla formazione del diritto consuetudinario in Francia (XIII–XVI)*, Milan, 1969

Dumas, A., *Histoire des obligations dans l'ancien droit français*, Aix-en-Provence, 1972

Ellul, J., *Histoire des institutions*, Paris, 1961–9; 5 vols.

Foviaux, J., *De l'Empire romain à la féodalité*, Paris, 1986; Droit et Institutions, I

Garaud, M., *Histoire générale du droit privé français (de 1789 à 1804)*, I: *La Révolution et l'égalité civile*, II: *La Révolution et la propriété foncière*, Paris, 1953–8

Garaud, M. and Szramkiewicz, R., *La Révolution française et la famille*, Paris, 1978; Publications Fac. Droit et Sciences Sociales Poitiers, 7

Gazzaniga, J.-L., *Introduction historique au droit des obligations*, Paris, 1992

Giffard, A. E., *Droit romain et ancien droit français. Les obligations*, 2nd edn, Paris, 1967; Précis Dalloz

Gläser, M., *Lehre und Rechtsprechung im französischen Zivilrecht des 19. Jahrhunderts*, Frankfurt, 1996; Ius Commune. Sonderhefte, 81

Gouron, A. and Rigaudière, A. (eds.), *Renaissance du pouvoir législatif et genèse de l'état*, Montpellier, 1987; Publ. Soc. Hist. Droit et Institutions Anciens Pays de Droit Ecrit, III [Collection of seventeen papers]

Guenée, B., *Tribunaux et gens de justice dans le bailliage de Senlis à la fin du moyen âge (vers 1350–1550)*, Paris, 1963

Guillot, O., Rigaudière, A. and Sassier, J., *Pouvoirs et institutions dans la France médiévale*, I: *Des origines à l'époque féodale*, II: *Des temps féodaux aux temps de l'Etat*, Paris, 1994; 2 vols.

Halpérin, J.-L., *Le Tribunal de Cassation et les pouvoirs sous la Révolution (1790–1799)*, Paris, 1987; Bibliothèque d'Histoire du Droit et Droit Romain (ed. by P. Timbal), XXIII

Histoire du droit privé français depuis 1804, Paris, 1996; Coll. Droit Fondamental

L'Impossible Code civil, Paris, 1992

Hilaire, J., *Introduction historique au droit commercial*, Paris, 1986; Coll. Droit Fondamental (ed. by S. Rials)

La Vie du droit. Coutumes et droit écrit, Paris, 1994

Hufteau, Y. L., *Le référé législatif et les pouvoirs du juge dans le silence de la loi*, Paris, 1965

Kelley, D. R., *Foundations of modern historical scholarship. Language, law and history in the French renaissance*, New York and London, 1970

Historians and the law in post-revolutionary France, Princeton, 1984

Krymen, J. and Rigaudière, A. (eds.), *Droits savants et pratiques françaises du pouvoir (XIe–XVe s.)*, Bordeaux, 1992

Lefebvre-Teillard, A., *Introduction historique au droit des personnes et de la famille*, Paris, 1996; Coll. Droit Fondamental

Lepointe, G., *Droit romain et ancien droit français. Les Biens; Régimes matrimoniaux, libéralités, successions; Les Obligations en ancien droit français*, Paris, 1958; 3 vols.

Leuwers, H., *Un juriste en politique. Merlin de Douai (1754–1838)*, Arras, 1996

Magnou-Nortier, E. (ed.), *Pouvoirs et libertés au temps des premiers Capétiens*, Maulevrier, 1992

Martin, X., *Nature humaine et Révolution française. Du siècle des Lumières au Code Napoléon*, Bouère, 1994

Musset, J., *Les régimes des biens entre époux en droit normand du VIe siècle à la Révolution française*, Caen, 1997

Naissance du Code civil an VII – an XII, 1800–1804, Paris, 1989

Olivier-Martin, F., *Histoire de la coutume de la prévôté et vicomté de Paris*, Paris, 1922–1930 (I, II 1 and 2); 3 vols. [Reprinted with a new bibliography by M. Boulet-Sautel, 1973]

Histoire du droit français des origines à la Révolution, Paris, 1948

Ourliac, P. and Gazzaniga, J.-L., *Histoire du droit privé français de l'An mil au Code civil*, Paris, 1985; Coll. Evolution de l'Humanité (fondée par H. Berr)

Ourliac, P. and Malafosse, J. de, *Histoire du droit privé*, I: *Les Obligations*, 2nd edn, Paris, 1969; II: *Les Biens*, 2nd edn, Paris, 1971; III: *Le Droit familial*, Paris, 1968; Thémis, Manuels Juridiques

Patault, A.-M., *Introduction historique au droit des biens*, Paris, 1989

Pegues, F. J., *The lawyers of the last Capetians*, Princeton, 1962

Petot, P., *Histoire du droit privé français. La Famille*, ed. by C. Bontems, Paris, 1993

Plesser, M. A., *Jean Etienne Marie Portalis und der Code civil*, Berlin, 1997; Freiburger Rechtsgeschichtliche Abhandlungen, new series, 28

Ramoz Núñez, B., *El código napoleónico y su recepción en América latina*, Lima, 1997

Raynal, J., *Histoire des institutions judiciaires*, Paris, 1964; Coll. Armand Colin, 381

Rogister, J., *Louis XV and the Parlement of Paris, 1737–1755*, Cambridge, 1995

Rousselet, M., *Histoire de la magistrature française des origines à nos jours*, Paris, 1957; 2 vols.

Royer, J.-P., *La société judiciaire depuis le XVIIIe siècle*, Paris, 1979
Histoire de la justice en France, 2nd edn, Paris, 1996; Coll. Droit Fondamental

Schulze, R. (ed.), *Französisches Zivilrecht in Europa während des 19. Jahrhunderts*, Berlin, 1994; Schriften zur Europäischen Rechts- und Verfassungsgeschichte, 12 [Collection of eleven articles concerning France, Germany, Holland, Italy, Poland, Spain and England]

Storez, I., *Le Chancelier Henri François d'Aguesseau (1668–1751), monarchiste et libéral*, Paris, 1996

Szramkiewicz, R., *Histoire du droit français de la famille*, Paris, 1995

Theewen, E. M., *Napoleons Anteil am Code civil*, Berlin, 1971; Schriften zur Europäischen Rechts- und Verfassungsgeschichte, 2

Thireau, J.-L., *Charles du Moulin (1500–1566). Etudes sur les sources, la méthode, les idées politiques et économiques d'un juriste de la Renaissance*, Geneva, 1980; Travaux d'Humanisme et Renaissance, 176

Timbal, P. C., *Les obligations contractuelles dans le droit français des XIIIe et XIVe siècles d'après la jurisprudence du Parlement*, Paris, 1973–7; 2 vols.; Centre d'Etude d'Histoire Juridique
Droit romain et ancien droit français. Régimes matrimoniaux, successions, libéralités, 2nd edn, Paris, 1975; Précis Dalloz

Tisset, P. and Ourliac, P., *Manuel d'histoire du droit*, Paris, 1949
Villers, R. and Giffard, A. E., *Droit romain et ancien droit français. Les Obligations*, Paris, 1958; Précis Dalloz

GERMANY, AUSTRIA, SWITZERLAND

Ahcin, C., *Zur Entstehung des bürgerlichen Gesetzbuchs für das Königreich Sachsen von 1863/65*, Frankfurt, 1996; Ius Commune. Sonderhefte, 85
Amira, K. von, *Grundriss des germanischen Rechts*, 4th edn by K. A. Eckhardt, I: *Rechtsdenkmäler*, II: *Rechtsaltertümer*, Berlin, 1960–7; Grundriss der Germanischen Philologie, 5, 1, 2
Anderson, D. L., *The Academy for German Law 1933–1944*, Michigan, 1982, Diss.; 2 vols.
Baltl, H., *Österreichische Rechtsgeschichte. Von den Anfängen bis zur Gegenwart*, 3rd edn, Graz, 1977
Baums, T. (ed.), *Entwurf eines allgemeinen Handelsgesetzbuches für Deutschland (1848–49). Text und Materialien*, Heidelberg, 1982
Becker, C., *Die Lehre von der laesio enormis in der Sicht der heutigen Wucherproblematik. Ausgewogenheit und § 138 BGB*, Cologne, 1993; Beiträge zur Neueren Privatrechtsgeschichte, 10
Behrends, O. (ed.), *Rudolf von Jhering. Beiträge und Zeugnisse aus Anlass der einhundersten Wiederkehr seines Todestages*, Göttingen, 1992
Jherings Rechtsdenken. Theorie und Pragmatik im Dienste evolutionärer Rechtsethik, Göttingen, 1996; Abh. Akad. Wiss. Göttingen. Philol.-hist. Kl., 3rd series, 216
Bender, P., *Die Rezeption des römischen Rechts im Urteil der deutschen Rechtswissenschaft*, Frankfurt, 1979; Rechtshistorische Reihe, 8
Bernard, P. P., *The limits of enlightenment. Joseph II and the law*, Urbana, Chicago, London, 1979
Björne, L., *Deutsche Rechtssysteme im 18. und 19. Jahrhundert*, Ebelsbach, 1984; Münchener Universitätsschriften. Jur. Fakultät. Abhandlungen zur Rechtswissenschaftlichen Grundlagenforschung, 59
Blasius, D., *Ehescheidung in Deutschland 1794–1945. Scheidung und Scheidungsrecht in historischer Perspektive*, Göttingen, 1987; Kritische Studien zur Geschichtswissenschaft, 74
Brandt, D., *Die politischen Parteien und die Vorlage des Bürgerlichen Gesetzbuches im Reichstag*, Heidelberg, 1975
Brun, G., *Leben und Werk des Rechtshistorikers Heinrich Mitteis unter besonderer Berücksichtigung seines Verhältnisses zum Nationalsozialismus*, Frankfurt, 1991

Caroni, P. (ed.), *Das Obligationenrecht 1883–1983. Berner Ringvorlesung zum Jubiläum des schweizerischen Obligationenrechts*, Berne and Stuttgart, 1984

Coing, H., *Epochen der Rechtsgeschichte in Deutschland*, 2nd edn, Munich, 1972

Vorträge zum 200. Geburtstag von F. C. von Savigny, Frankfurt, 1979; Ius Commune, 8

Coing, H. and Wilhelm, W. (eds.), *Wissenschaft und Kodifikation des Privatrechts im 19. Jahrhundert*, Frankfurt, 1974–82; 6 vols.; Studien zur Rechtswissenschaft des 19. Jahrhunderts

Conrad, H., *Deutsche Rechtsgeschichte*, I: *Frühzeit und Mittelalter*, 2nd edn, Karlsruhe, 1962, II: *Neuzeit bis 1806*, 1966

Dahlmanns, G. J., *Strukturwandel des deutschen Zivilprozesses im 19. Jahrhundert*, Aalen, 1971

Dannreuther, D., *Der Zivilprozess als Gegenstand der Rechtspolitik im deutschen Reich 1871–1945. Ein Beitrag zur Geschichte des Zivilprozessrechts in Deutschland*, Frankfurt, 1987; Rechtshistorische Reihe, 53

Dilcher, G. *et al.*, *Gewohnheitsrecht und Rechtsgewohnheiten im Mittelalter*, Berlin, 1992; Schriften zur Europäischen Rechts- und Verfassungsgeschichte, 6

Dölemeyer, B. and Mohnhaupt, H. (eds.), *200 Jahre Allgemeines Landrecht für die Preussischen Staaten. Wirkungsgeschichte und internationaler Kontext*, Frankfurt, 1995; Ius Commune. Sonderhefte, 75

Ebel, F., *200 Jahre preussischer Zivilprozess. Das Corpus iuris Fridericianum vom Jahre 1781*, Berlin and New York, 1982; Schriftenreihe der Juristischen Gesellschaft zu Berlin, 71

Savigny officialis, Berlin and New York, 1987; Schriftenreihe der Juristischen Gesellschaft zu Berlin, 104

Rechtsgeschichte. Ein Lehrbuch, I: *Antike und Mittelalter*, II: *Neuzeit*, Heidelberg, 1989–93

Ebel, W., *Geschichte der Gesetzgebung in Deutschland*, 2nd edn by F. Ebel, Göttingen, 1988; Göttinger Rechtswissenschaftliche Studien, 24

Eisenhardt, U., *Deutsche Rechtsgeschichte*, Munich, 1984

Elsener, F. (ed.), *Lebensbilder zur Geschichte der Tübinger Juristenfakultät*, Tübingen, 1977

Faussner, H. C. *et al.*, *Die österreichische Rechtsgeschichte. Standortbestimmung und Zukunftperspektiven*, Graz, 1991; Grazer Rechts- und Staatswiss. Studien, 47

Flossmann, H., *Österreichische Privatrechtsgeschichte*, 3rd edn, Vienna, New York, 1996; Springers Kurzlehrbücher der Rechtswissenschaft

Gmür, R., *Grundriss der deutschen Rechtsgeschichte*, 2nd edn, Bielefeld, 1 980; Juristische Arbeitsblätter, Sonderhefte, 2

Grahl, C., *Die Abschaffung der Advocatur unter Friedrich dem Grossen. Prozessbetrieb und Parteibeistand im preussischen Zivilgerichtsverfahren bis zum Ende des 1 8. Jahrhunderts*, Göttingen, 1 994; Quellen und Forschungen zum Recht und seiner Geschichte, 2

Hagemann, H. R., *Basler Rechtsleben im Mittelalter*, Basle, 1 981–7; 2 vols.

Hahn, E. J., *Rudolf von Gneist. Ein politischer Jurist*, Frankfurt, 1 995; Ius Commune. Sonderhefte, 74

Hattenhauer, H., *Zur Geschichte der deutschen Rechts- und Gesetzessprache*, Göttingen, 1 987; Berichte aus den Sitzungen der J. Jungius-Gesellschaft, Hamburg, V, 2

Die geistesgeschichtlichen Grundlagen des deutschen Rechts, 4th edn, Heidelberg, 1 996; Uni-Taschenbücher, 1 042

Hofmeister, H. (ed.), *Kodifikation als Mittel der Politik. Vorträge und Diskussionsbeiträge über die deutsche, schweizerische und österreichische Kodifikationsbewegung um 1 900*, Graz, Cologne, 1 986; Wiener Rechtsgeschichtliche Arbeiten, 1 6

Hoke, R., *Österreichische und Deutsche Rechtsgeschichte*, Vienna, Cologne, Weimar, 1 992

Quellensammlung zur österreichischen und deutschen Rechtsgeschichte, Vienna, Cologne, Weimar, 1 993

Holthöfer, E., *Ein deutscher Weg zu moderner und rechtsstaatlicher Gerichtsverfassung. Das Beispiel Württemberg*, Stuttgart, 1 997

Jakobs, H., *Wissenschaft und Gesetzgebung im bürgerlichen Recht nach der Rechtsquellenlehre des 1 9. Jahrhunderts*, Paderborn, 1 983; Rechts- und Staatswissenschaftliche Veröffentlichungen der Görres-Gesellschaft, n.s. 38

Janssen, A., *Otto von Gierkes Methode der geschichtlichen Rechtswissenschaft. Studien zu den Wegen und Formen seines juristischen Denkens*, Göttingen, 1 974; Göttinger Studien zur Rechtsgeschichte (ed. K. Kroeschell), 8

Jayme, E. and Mansel, H.-P. (eds.), *Auf dem Wege zu einem gemeineuropäischen Privatrecht. 1 00 Jahre BGB und die lusophonen Länder*, Baden-Baden, 1 997

John, M., *Politics and the law in late nineteenth-century Germany. The origins of the civil code*, Oxford, 1 989

Kaufmann, E., *Deutsches Recht. Die Grundlagen*, Berlin, Bielefeld, Munich, 1 986; Grundlagen der Germanistik, 27

Kern, B.-R., *Georg Beseler. Leben und Werk*, Berlin, 1982; Schriften zur Rechtsgeschichte, 26

Kern, E., *Geschichte des Gerichtsverfassungsrechts*, Munich, Berlin, 1954

Köbler, G., *Das Recht im frühen Mittelalter*, Cologne, Vienna, 1971; Forschungen zur Deutschen Rechtsgeschichte, 7

Deutsche Rechtsgeschichte. Ein systematischer Grundriss der geschichtlichen Grundlagen des deutschen Rechts von den Indogermanen bis zur Gegenwart, 4th edn, Munich, 1990

Kroeschell, K., *Deutsche Rechtsgeschichte*, I: *Bis 1250*, II: *1250–1650*, III: *Seit 1650*, Hamburg, 1972–89

Rechtsgeschichte Deutschlands im 20. Jahrhundert, Göttingen, 1992; Uni-Taschenbücher, 1681

Landau, P., Nehlsen, H. and Willoweit, D., (eds.), *Heinrich Mitteis nach hundert Jahren (1889–1989)*, Munich, 1991; Bayer. Akad. Wiss., Philos. Hist., Kl. Abh. N.F., 106

Laufs, A., *Rechtsentwicklungen in Deutschland*, 5th edn, Berlin, New York, 1996

Lehner, O., *Familie, Recht, Politik. Die Entwicklung des österreichischen Familienrechts im 19. und 20. Jahrhundert*, Vienna, New York, 1987

Loschelder, M., *Die österreichische allgemeine Gerichtsordnung von 1781. Grundlagen und Kodifikationsgeschichte*, Berlin, 1978; Schriften zur Rechtsgeschichte, 18

Marini, G. (ed.), *A. F. J. Thibaut – F. C. Savigny. La polemica sulla codificazione*, Naples, 1982

Mitteis, H., *Deutsche Rechtsgeschichte. Ein Studienbuch*, 14th edn by H. Lieberich, Berlin, 1976

Motte, O., *Savigny et la France*, Berne, 1983

Nörr, D., *Savignys philosophische Lehrjahre*, Frankfurt, 1994

Nörr, K. W., *Reinhardt und die Revision der allegemeinen Gerichtsordnung für die preussischen Staaten. Materialien zur Reform des Zivilprozesses im 19. Jahrhundert*, Frankfurt, 1975; Ius Commune. Sonderhefte, 4

Zwischen den Mühlsteinen. Eine Privatrechtsgeschichte der Weimarer Republik, Tübingen, 1988

Eher Hegel als Kant. Zum Privatrechtsverständnis im 19. Jahrhundert, Paderborn, 1991; Rechts- und Staatswissenschaftliche Veröff. der Görres-Gesellschaft, new series, 589

Ogorek, R., *Richterkönig oder Subsumtionsautomat? Zur Justiztheorie im 19. Jahrhundert*, Frankfurt, 1986; Rechtsprechung: Materialien und Studien. Veröffentlichungen des Max-Planck-Instituts für Europäische Rechtsgeschichte, 1

Ogris, W., *Die Rechtsentwicklung in Österreich 1848–1918*, Vienna, 1970

Oppitz, U.-D., *Deutsche Rechtsbücher des Mittelalters*, I: *Beschreibung der Rechtsbücher*, II: *Beschreibung der Handschriften*, III: *Abbildungen und Fragmente*, Cologne, Vienna, 1991–3

Pichinot, H.-R., *Die Akademie für deutsches Recht. Aufbau und Entwicklung einer öffentlich-rechtlichen Körperschaft des Dritten Reiches*, Kiel, 1981

Pick, E., *Aufklärung und Erneuerung des juristischen Studiums. Verfassung. Studium und Reform in Dokumenten am Beispiel der Mainzer Fakultät gegen Ende des Ancien Régime*, Berlin and Munich, 1983; Historische Forschungen, 24

Planitz, H., *Deutsche Rechtsgeschichte*, 3rd edn by K. A. Eckhardt, Graz, Cologne, 1971

Rückert, J., *Idealismus, Jurisprudenz und Politik bei F. C. von Savigny*, Ebelsbach, 1984

Rückert, J. and Willoweit, D. (eds.), *Die deutsche Rechtsgeschichte in der NS-Zeit. Ihre Vorgeschichte und Nachwirkung*, Tübingen, 1995

Rüthers, B., *Entartetes Recht. Rechtslehren und Kronjuristen im Dritten Reich*, Munich, 1994

Schlosser, H., *Grundzüge der neueren Privatrechtsgeschichte. Ein Studienbuch*, 8th edn, Heidelberg, 1996; Uni-Taschenbuch, 882

Schmidt, K., *Einhundert Jahre Verbandstheorie im Privatrecht. Aktuelle Betrachtungen zur Wirkungsgeschichte von Otto von Gierkes Genossenschaftstheorie*, Göttingen, 1987

Schott, C., *Rat und Spruch der Juristischen Fakultät Freiburg im Breisgau*, Freiburg, 1965

Schröder, H., *Friedrich Karl von Savigny. Geschichte und Rechtsdenken beim Übergang vom Feudalismus zum Kapitalismus in Deutschland*, Frankfurt, Berne, New York, 1984

Schubert, W. (ed.), *Entstehung und Quellen der Zivilprozessordnung von 1877*, Frankfurt, 1987; 2 vols.; Ius Commune. Sonderhefte, 34

Schubert, W., Schmiedel, B. and Krampe, C. (eds.), *Quellen zum Handelsgesetzbuch von 1897*, I: *Gesetze und Entwürfe*, II, 1,2: *Denkschriften, Beratungen, Berichte*, Frankfurt, 1986

Schudnagies, C., *Hans Frank. Aufstieg und Fall des NS-Juristen und Generalgouverneurs*, Frankfurt, Bern, 1989; Rechtshistorische Reihe, 67

Schulte-Nölke, H., *Das Reichsjustizamt und die Entstehung des Bürgerlichen Gesetzbuchs*, Frankfurt, 1995; Ius Commune. Sonderhefte, 71

Schwennicke, A., *Die Entstehung der Einleitung des Preussichen Allgemeinen Landrechts von 1794*, Frankfurt, 1993; Ius Commune. Sonderhefte, 6

Schwerin, C., von, *Grundzüge der deutschen Rechtsgeschichte*, 4th edn by H. Thieme, Berlin and Munich, 1950

Scovazzi, M., *Le origini del diritto germanico. Fonti, preistoria, diritto pubblico*, Milan, 1957

Simon, W., *Claudius Freiherr von Schwerin. Rechtshistoriker während dreier Epochen deutscher Geschichte*, Frankfurt, 1991

Stelzer, W., *Gelehrtes Recht in Österreich von den Anfängen bis zum frühen 14. Jahrhundert*, Vienna, 1982

Stolleis, M., *Recht im Unrecht. Studien zur Rechtsgeschichte des Nationalsozialismus*, Frankfurt, 1994

Stolleis, M. and Simon, D. (eds.), *Rechtsgeschichte im Nationalsozialismus*, Tübingen, 1989

Thibaut und Savigny. Ein programmatischer Rechtsstreit, Darmstadt, 1959

Thieme, H., *Ideengeschichte und Rechtsgeschichte. Gesammelte Schriften*, Cologne, Vienna, 1986; 2 vols.; Forschungen zur Neueren Privatrechtsgeschichte, 25/I, II

Tripp, D., *Der Einfluss des naturwissenschaftlichen, philosophischen und historischen Positivismus auf die deutsche Rechtslehre im 19. Jahrhundert*, Berlin, 1983; Schriften zur Rechtsgeschichte, 31

Vormbaum, T., *Sozialdemokratie und Zivilrechtskodifikation*, Berlin, New York, 1977

Weitzel, J., *Dinggenossenschaft und Recht. Untersuchungen zum Rechtsverständnis im fränkisch-deutschen Mittelalter*, Cologne, 1985; 2 vols.; Quellen und Forschungen zur Höchsten Gerichtsbarkeit im Alten Reich, 15, I, II

Welker, K. H. L., *Rechtsgeschichte als Rechtspolitik. Justus Möser als Jurist und Staatsmann*, Osnabrück, 1996

Wesenberg, G., *Neuere deutsche Privatrechtsgeschichte im Rahmen der europäischen Rechtsentwicklung*, 3rd edn by G. Wesener, Lahr, 1976

Wesener, G., *Einflüsse und Geltung des römisch-gemeinen Rechts in den altösterreichischen Ländern in der Neuzeit (16. bis 18. Jahrhundert)*, Vienna, 1989; Forschungen zur Neueren Privatrechtsgeschichte, 27

Whitman, J. Q., *The legacy of Roman law in the German romantic era. Historical vision and legal change*, Princeton, 1990

Wieacker, F., *Rudolf von Jhering. Eine Erinnerung zum 50. Todestage*, Leipzig, 1942

Wiegand, W., *Studien zur Rechtsanwendungslehre der Rezeptionszeit*, Ebelsbach, 1977

ITALY

Amelio, M. d', *Illuminismo e scienza del diritto in Italia*, Milan, 1965

Astuti, G., *Lezioni di storia del diritto italiano. Le fonti. Età romano-barbarica*, Padua, 1953

Bellomo, M., *Società e istituzioni in Italia tra medioevo ed età moderna*, 4th edn, Rome, 1987

Besta, E., *Avviamento allo studio della storia del diritto italiano*, 2nd edn, Milan, 1946

Fonti del diritto italiano dalla caduta dell'Impero Romano sino ai tempi nostri, 2nd edn, Milan, 1950

Bognetti, G. P., *L'età Longobarda*, Milan, 1966–8; 4 vols.

Bonini, R., *Disegno storico del diritto privato italiano dal Codice civile del 1865 al Codice civile de 1942*, 3rd edn, Bologna, 1996; Studi e Materiali per gli Insegnamenti Storico-giuridici, 1

Il diritto privato dal nuovo secolo alla prima guerra mondiale. Linee di storia giuridica italiana ed europea, Bologna, 1996; Studi e Materiali per gli Insegnamenti Storico-giuridici, 12

Bougard, F., *La justice dans le royaume d'Italie de la fin du VIIIe siècle au début du XIe siècle*, Rome, 1995; Bibliothèque des Ecoles Françaises d'Athènes et de Rome, 291

Diurni, G., *Le situazioni possessorie nel medioevo. Età longobardo-franca*, Milan, 1988; Quaderni di Studi Senesi, 64

Fried, J., *Die Entstehung des Juristenstandes im 12. Jahrhundert. Zur sozialen Stellung und politischen Bedeutung gelehrter Juristen in Bologna und Modena*, Cologne and Vienna, 1974; Forschungen zur Neueren Privatrechtsgeschichte, 21

Leicht, P. S., *Storia del diritto italiano. Le fonti*, 3rd edn, Milan, 1947

Martines, L., *Lawyers and statecraft in Renaissance Florence*, Princeton, 1968

Zorzoli, M. C., *Università dottori giureconsulti. L'organizzazione della 'facoltà legale' di Pavia nell'età Spagnola*, Padua, 1986; Publ. Univ. Pavia. Studi nelle Scienze Giuridiche e Sociali, n.s. 46

SPAIN

Clavero, B. *et al.* (eds.), *Hispania. Entre derechos proprios y derechos nacionales*, Milan, 1990; 2 vols.

Galto Fernández, E., Alejandre García, J. A. and García Marín, J. M., *El derecho histórico de los pueblos de España*, 3rd edn, Madrid, 1982

García-Gallo, A., *Manual de historia del derecho español*, 8th edn, Madrid, 1978; 2 vols.
Gibert, R., *Historia general del derecho español*, Granada, 1968
Iglesia Ferreiros, A., *La creación del derecho. Una historia de la formación de un derecho estatal español*, Barcelona, 1992; 2 vols.
Lalinde Abadia, J., *Iniciación histórica al derecho español*, 3rd edn, Barcelona, 1983
Peláez, M. J., *Trabajos de historia del derecho privado*, Barcelona, 1993
Pérez-Prendes, J. M., *Curso de historia del derecho español*, Madrid, 1973
Tomás y Valiente, F., *Manual de historia del derecho español*, 3rd edn, Madrid, 1981

BIBLIOGRAPHIES AND DICTIONARIES

Deutsches Rechtswörterbuch. Wörterbuch der älteren deutschen Rechtssprache, ed. by R. Schröder and E. von Künssberg, Weimar, 1914 ff.
Gilissen, J. (ed.), *Introduction bibliographique à l'histoire du droit et à l'ethnologie juridique*, Brussels, 1964–88; 9 vols.
Handwörterbuch zur deutschen Rechtsgeschichte, ed. by A. Erler and E. Kaufmann, Berlin, 1964–98; 5 vols.
Hattum, M. van and Rooseboom, H., *Glossarium van oude Nederlandse rechtstermen*, Amsterdam, 1977
Köbler, G., *Etymologisches Rechtswörterbuch*, Tübingen, 1995; Uni-Taschenbücher, 1988
Einfache Bibliographie europäisch-deutscher Rechtsgeschichte, Giessen, 1990; Arbeiten zur Rechts- und Sprachwissenschaft, 29
Lepointe, G. and Vandenbossche, A. (eds.), *Eléments de bibliographie sur l'histoire des institutions et des faits sociaux (987–1875)*, Paris, 1958
Planitz, H. and Buyken, T., *Bibliographie zur deutschen Rechtsgeschichte*, Frankfurt, 1952; 2 vols.
Ragueau, F. and de Laurière, E., *Glossaire du droit français*, 2nd edn by L. Favre, Niort, 1882
Stallaert, K., *Glossarium van verouderde rechtstermen*, Leiden, 1886–(1893) (to *poer*), 2 vols; vol. III by F. Debrabandere (*P–W*), Handzame, 1977

Index

administrative law. *See* judicial review;
        public/private law dichotomy
Anglo-Norman feudal law, 2–3
    briefs (*brevia*), 2
    See also Normandy
Aristotle, 80
Australia
    annexation of aboriginal lands,
        original intent/evolving
        standards dilemma, 59–60
    judicial law-making, 61–2
    natural justice, 61

Belgium
    judicial role, dissenting opinions, 45
    scholarship and education, role, 45
briefs (*brevia*), 2

canon law
    as a common law of western Europe,
        14
    as a set of norms, 14
    continuing effect post-Reformation,
        14–15
    in England, 15, 20–1
    Roman law basis, 13–14
        ecclesia vivit lege Romana, 13–14
    twelfth-century systematization, 14
Church (medieval)
    centralized structure, 16, 24, 76,
        140
        Roman Empire influences, 14, 78,
            141
        synodal system and, 140
    courts. *See* Church courts (medieval)
    financial organization, 15–16
    government by Council (14th–15th
        century), 16

Papal supremacy, 78–9
    a quasi-European State, 15–17
    role of State distinguished, 16–17
    See also canon law
Church courts (medieval), 15
    competence
        orthodoxy/heresy questions, 15
        ratione materiae, 15, 24
        ratione personae (clerics), 15, 24
    composition, 78
    inquisitorial system, 51–2
    procedural law, 48–9
    State's enforcement role, 15
codification
    'code' distinguished, 39–40
    French commercial customary law, 81
    See also England, codification;
            Germany, codification debate
'common law' defined
    as expression of political unity, 34
    droit commun, 14
    droit commun français, 14, 34
    English 'common law', 14, 34
    Gemeines Recht, 14, 34
    ius commune, 14
    See also common law/civil law
            divergence/convergence
common law/civil law
        divergence/convergence
    adversarial/inquistorial approach, 51–3
    codification and, 39–41, 90–2
    conceptual bases, 33
    English aversion to codification, 33,
        40–1
    judicial role, 44–5
        dissenting opinions, 45
    language difficulties and, 31
    mentalités at odds, 32

168

as 'holy writ', 55, 62–72
as 'old' law, 71–2
conservative nature, 68
drafting
  absence of legislature, 676
  Cambacérès's Projects, 65, 66, 67
  Council of State and, 68
  judicial involvement, 68
  Napoleon's role, 68
in Germany, 64
influence of scholars, 34
interpretation
  ancient customs and ordinances,
    71–2
  exegesis, 22, 63–4, 68–72
  natural law, 71
  original intent, 70
  preparatory texts as aid, 70
political nature, 64–9
popularity, 99
unifying influence, 67
codification of customary commercial
  law, 81
Custom of Paris (*coutume de Paris*), 3–4,
  85
Dumoulin's commentaries, 24
customary law, relevance, 93–4
dotal system 4, 72 n. 41
droit commun, definition, 14
droit commun français, 34
  definition, 14
influence on Japan, 6
influences
  German customary law, 3–4
  Roman law, 3–4
  attempted abolition, 8–10
  synthesis, 4
Napoleonic changes
  a clean break?, 9–10
  divorce, 65–6
  illegitimate children, status, 66
  See also Civil Procedure Code; *Code
    civil* 1804
natural law, 69, 71
north/south divide, 3–4, 35, 72 n. 41
pays de droit coutumier, 3
pays de droit écrit, 3
régime de la communauté, 4 n. 2
scholarship and education, role, 6, 9,
  34, 45
Ecole de Magistrature, 47

legists under Philip IV the Fair, 77
substantive/procedural law dichotomy,
  48
See also Normandy
fungible persons, 44

general principles of law, unification of
  European law and, 29
Germany
  1495 developments, 5–6
  a clean break?, 7–8
  Civil Code (*BGB*) 1896/1900, 34
    adoption by Japan, 6–7
    customary law and, 34–5, 92–4
    influence of scholars, 34, 35, 98–9
    popularity of French *Code civil*
      compared, 99
    Roman law influence, 4–5, 6–7, 34
    Volksgesetzbuch and. *See* Nazi attitude
  codification debate
    Germanists and Romanists, 8, 92–4
    political underpinnings, 91–2, 99
    Savigny/Thibaut (*Professorenstreit*),
      91–2
    von Gierke's criticisms, 95–6, 98–9
    See also Civil Code (*BGB*)
      1896/1900
  courts in
    Reichskammergericht (instituted 1495),
      5–6
    legal qualifications, 5
    membership, 5
    Schöffengerichte (aldermen's courts), 6
  gemeines Recht ('common law'), 94, 139
    1495 developments, 5–6
    definition, 14, 128–9
  Genossenschaftsrecht, 95
  influences
    French Napoleonic Code, 64, 94 n. 6
    ius commune, 25
    Roman law, 4–6, 34–5
    calls for rejection of, 100–3.
    See also Nazi attitudes
  Kaiserrecht, 5, 7–8
  Pandektenrecht (Pandectists), 8, 25,
    34, 38, 90, 95–6, 99, 110, 139
  Rezeption, 5–6, 17
  usus modernus, 34, 95–6
  inquisitorial system
    Assistenzräte, 52
    Instrukstions/Offizialmaxime., 52

natural law (*cont.*)
  France, 69
  Germany, 92
  Netherlands, Civil Code (New),
    introduction, 1, 33
Normandy
  influence on English law, 2
  Roman law in, 2–3, 4 n. 2
  See also Anglo-Norman law; France
novitates, 11, 63

Papal States, 15 n. 15
private law, of the future, 136–40
procedural law
  autonomous nature, 48–50
  Church courts, 48–9
  England, 9–50
  France, 48
  Germany, 48
  ius commune, 48–9
  Justinian, 48
  possibilities for harmonization, 31
  Roman law, 48
  Russia, 48
property law, harmonization proposals,
  30
public/private law dichotomy
  common law, 41–2
  prestige of private law, 43–4
  Roman law, 43
  socialist countries, 43
  twentieth century, 43–4
  See also judicial review

Renaissance (twelfth Century), 79–80
Roman Dutch law, 25
  English law influence, 140
Roman law
  customary basis, 56
  ius privatum/ius publicum dichotomy,
    43
  procedural law, 48
  res fungibilis, 44
Roman law influence in
  canon law, 13–14
  ECJ case law, 30
  England, 38–9
  France, 3–4
  Germany, 4–6, 7–8, 17, 92–7
  Japan, 6–7, 139

Louisiana, 34
Normandy, 2–3, 4 n. 2
unification of European law, 28, 30
  See also ius commune; Justinian (*Corpus juris civilis*)
Russia, procedural law, 48

Salic law, 3
  Karl August Eckhardt's 1962/1969
    edition, 122–3
sanctity of the written law
  American Declaration of
    Independence, 55
  English statute law, 54
  exegesis, definition, 62–3
  French *Code civil* 1804, 55, 62–72
  interpretative problems, 55–6
    acceptable sources, 64
    original intent/evolving standards
      dilemma, 56–60
    School of Exegesis/Scientific
      School, 22, 63–4, 68–72
    whose standards?, 60
  rules of construction and, 54
  ius commune, 54–6
  novitates, 11, 63
  US Constitution, 56–62
scholarship and education, role
  Belgium, 45
  England, 46–8
  France, 9, 45, 47, 77–8
  Germany, 34–5, 45–6
  Holy Roman Empire
    Constitutio Habita, 76
    foundation of University of Naples
      (1224), 77
  ius commune, 7–8, 13, 17, 20–1, 24,
    75–9, 81–2
  unification of European law, 27,
    34–5
scholarship. *See* scholarship and
  education, role
Scotland, *ius commune* and, 140
social concerns
  Germany, 95–7
  Russia, 97
  Social Chapter (Treaty of Maastricht),
    96–7
South Africa, *ius commune* and, 140
Spain, *ius commune* and, 140